The Magic Presence™

"I AM" ADORATIONS AND AFFIRMATIONS

PART I

"I AM" DECREES

PART II

"I AM" ACTIVITY
OF
SAINT GERMAIN FOUNDATION

The "I AM" Activity represents the Original, Permanent, and Highest Source of the Ascended Masters' Instruction on the Great Laws of Life, as first offered to the western world by the Ascended Master Saint Germain, through His Accredited Messengers, Mr. and Mrs. Guy W. Ballard.

In the early 1930s the Ballards established Saint Germain Foundation and Saint Germain Press, Inc., which under Saint Germain's Guidance, have expanded into worldwide organizations that offer to mankind the true Ascended Master Teachings on the Great Cosmic Words, "I AM"! Saint Germain Foundation strives to keep the "I AM" Ascended Master Instruction in Its pure, unadulterated form, free from any human interpretation, personal monetary gain, or proselytizing, as It is a Gift from the Great Ascended Masters and Cosmic Beings to bring Illumination and Perfection to mankind.

Hundreds of "I AM" Temples and Sanctuaries exist throughout the world, where the Teachings are applied in "I AM" Decree Groups. The Books of the Saint Germain Series are available in many libraries, bookstores, or directly from Saint Germain Press (address below). For further information, please contact:

SAINT GERMAIN FOUNDATION
SAINT GERMAIN PRESS
1120 Stonehedge Drive
Schaumburg, Illinois 60194 USA
(847) 882-7400 or (800) 662-2800
www.saintgermainfoundation.org
www.saintgermainpress.com

SAINT GERMAIN SERIES

VOLUME 5
Part I

"I AM" ADORATIONS AND AFFIRMATIONS

BY
CHANERA

SAINT GERMAIN PRESS

1998 Printing
Printed in the United States of America

Library of Congress Cataloging-in-Publication Data
Chanera, 1886-1971.
["I AM" adorations and affirmations]
"I AM" adorations and affirmations ; "I AM" decrees / by Chanera.
--3rd ed.
p. cm. -- (The Saint Germain series ; v. 5)
ISBN 1-878891-24-3
1. I AM Religious Activity. I. Chanera, 1886-1971. "I AM" decrees. II. Title: "I AM" adorations and affirmations.
III. Title: "I AM" decrees. IV. Series.
BP605.I18C47 1991
299' .93 -- dc20 91-20332
CIP

✧ ✧ ✧

CONTENTS

PART I

PART II

Decrees

DEDICATION

This series of Books is dedicated in Eternal Love and Gratitude to our Beloved Ascended Masters, Saint Germain, Jesus, Nada, the Great Divine Director, and also to the Great White Brotherhood, the Brotherhood at the Royal Teton, the Brotherhood of Mount Shasta, the Great Ones from Venus, and those other Ascended Masters whose loving help has been direct and without limit.

✧

✧✧✧

FOREWORD

At the request of many Students, this Book of "'I AM' Adorations and Affirmations" is given to the public. They are sent out with the Decree that: "All who read or use these Commands shall be held, by the Love of the 'Mighty I AM Presence,' in constant conscious communion with that Master Presence of Light within themselves."

Every time the Great Creative Word, "I AM"! is read, thought or spoken, the feeling released should be that of an exclamation because "I AM"! is the Life from the Great Central Sun announcing Its Presence through the individual who thinks, speaks or feels that Great Eternal Fiat of Life's existence. Therefore, always release that strong powerful feeling whenever you use the Great Creative Word, "I AM."

In this way, the limitless Energy of Life releases through you to fulfill your Call for assistance and Perfection.

If the Student will read these Decrees slowly and with deep, deep feeling in each word as you come to it, you will have Instantaneous Manifestations when you can feel the meaning in each Word deeply enough.

The word "human," throughout this Series of Books, is always used to mean discordant. When the word "annihilate" is used, it always means the annihilation of discord or imperfection, for no one can annihilate God, Good, Who is Life; and the annihilation of discord can only bring Happiness and Perfection as a result to all.

This Book is charged with and carries to Its readers the Rays of Light and Love from the Ascended Masters, Saint Germain, Jesus, Nada, the Great Divine Director, and the other Ascended Masters who are pouring Their Radiance through This Activity, to which Godfre Ray King, Lotus Ray King and Donald Ray King add their Triple Activity of Light and Love from the "Mighty I AM Presence" for the Illumination, Freedom, Mastery and Perfection of all who read or contact It, for America and the world.

Chanera

The first duty of the outer self is to turn to the "Beloved Mighty I AM Presence" and ask for orders.

"I AM"
ADORATIONS
AND
AFFIRMATIONS

✧

VOLUME 5
Part I

"I AM" ACKNOWLEDGMENT

The "Mighty I AM Presence" is within this Book! Let all of Earth keep silent before It and be at Peace, in humble, grateful, loving, adoring Obedience unto that blazing Light, our Supreme Source.

Keep us, O "Mighty I AM Presence," humble before Thee, positive to the world, and forever in the Service of the Ascended Host of Light.

All "I AM," or have, or ever hope to be or have is Thine, O "Mighty I AM Presence"! Come forth, in the Fullness of Thy Power! Control and hold Dominion in this body, brain, mind and will! Pour forth Thy Full Glory on Earth, as Thou art in Heaven! Do Thou so illumine me by Thy Light that there is none of me but all of Thee.

There is a "Presence" in man, and the Light from that Presence is his Understanding. That "Presence," that Light, and that Understanding is "I AM"; and "I AM" That "I AM"!

I call unto Thee, O "Mighty I AM Presence," Thou Great Central Sun, Thou Heart of Infinity! Pour forth Thy Mighty Flame of Divine Love throughout humanity and the Earth! Set the feet of mankind once again securely upon the Pathway of Light, and anchor their attention forever upon Thee, the Great Love Star in the Heart of each one! Lift their Hearts unto the Heights whence cometh all Help, and bring them back into the Happiness, Freedom and Perfection which is their birthright.

The "Mighty I AM Presence" is within this Holy Temple; let all of Earth keep silent before that Blazing Glory, and be at peace! in humble, grateful, loving, adoring obedience unto that Supreme Source.

O Presence of the Diamond Heart! come forth in the Fullness of Thy Power! Release Thy Victory everywhere, and seal all within Thy Heart, forever.

CLASS ACKNOWLEDGMENT

This Class (Group) is a "Temple of Light"!
The "Heart of Divine Love"!
The "Secret Breath of God"!
The "Altar of Eternal Peace"!
The "Focus of the Great Silence"!
The "Ocean of Limitless Power"!
The "Treasure Chest of the Almighty"!
The "Sun of Everlasting Freedom"!
The "Throne Room of Infinite Life"!
The "Gift of the 'Mighty I AM Presence,'" forever!

✦ *Note: The above can be used for healing the body, as well as for the Class Work.* ✦

In the Fullness of the "Presence"
Is the Love that you require,
In the Fullness of the "Presence"
Are the things that you desire!

✧✧✧

BROTHERS OF THE GOLDEN ROBE

Great Beings of the Golden Robe,
Transcendent Ones of Love!
Enfold all those upon the Earth
Who call to Thee above.

Guard well the children seeking Light,
Release through them Thy Power;
To those who know and need Thee, COME!
Be with them every hour.

Reveal the Glory of Thy Height,
The Victory Thou hast won,
Blaze forth Thy Full Dominion NOW,
Great Masters from the Sun.

Show all Thy Mantles of Love's Light
So golden hued and pure;
Enfold us, as we call to Thee,
And make our Victory sure!

Great Beings of the Golden Robe,
In Love's Own Sacred Name,
Awaken everyone on Earth
To LIGHT, the "Great I AM"!

THE DIAMOND HEART

O Presence of the Diamond Heart!
In Victory now I come,
Bearing the "Cup of Liquid Light,"
All Earth's battles won.
I raise my sword and now step through;
Within the Flame, I bow to You,
And You, the Heart of Light in all,
Reveal to me the Great, the small.
Upon my shoulders, blazing bright
You place my Cape of dazzling Light;
And I, at last, all blest and Free,
Know only Love, myself, as Thee.

O Presence of the Diamond Heart,
All Ecstasy Supreme;
Thy Joy now all encompassing,
My own Life's Radiant Stream,
Is ever pouring out Its Light–
All–All Perfection too;
"I AM"! Thy Presence, Lord of Life,
O Great Love Flame, just You!
In Love, in Peace, in Glorious Power,
In all realms and all space,
I hold Thy Hand, Thou Source of All,
"I AM"! Thy own Bright Face.

LORDS OF THE BLUE FLAME

Lords of the Flame, the Sacred Fire,
The Great, Great Ray of Blue!
Flood forth o'er our America,
Earth's atmosphere step through.

From Thy Great Heart of Love so pure,
Of Wisdom and ALL Power,
Blaze forth Thy Dazzling Cosmic Light,
Protect Her every hour!

Through Angel Host of Beings bright
Send forth the Great Blue Flame
To fill our loved America
With Victory, through "I AM"!

That Mighty Glorious Sacred Name,
For all Eternity,
Shall evermore now fill the Earth,
Till all mankind is Free!

"I AM"! says Life to all that is;
"I AM"! Love's Gift to all;
"I AM"! the Mighty Flame of Blue,
"I AM"! Its Cosmic Call!

THE LOVE STAR

THE LOVE STAR–*"The Secret"*

Love Star, Love Star, Love Star bright,
Love Star, Love Star, blaze through us Thy Might;
Love Star, Love Star, our own Hearts' Light!
Love Star, Love Star, enfold us tonight.

THE LOVE STAR–*"The Call"*

O Love Star! we call Thee,
Thou Jewel from the Sun,
O Heart of Creation,
Thou Glorious One!
Come now in Thy Splendor,
Flash forth Thy Great Flame,
Burst all bonds asunder,
Speak forth the Great Name!
Declare now Thy Victory
And set this Earth Free;

Reveal Thy Dominion,
Thyself let all see.
From Thy Blazing Altar,
Light's Greeting first came,
The Voice of God's "Presence,"
Almighty, "I AM"!

THE LOVE STAR–*"The Presence"*

The Love Star–His Presence!
All silent, serene,
In Glory transcendent
While blessing the scene;
Stands radiant with Power
Its Rays pulsing bright,
Chaste ribbons of silver
Adorning the night;
Caressing, encircling,
Enfolding the sod;
Light! tying the Earth to the
Feet of her God!
The Master Christ Presence,
Incarnate in man;
The Source of all Freedom,
The Blest Word, "I AM"!

✧

✧ ✧ ✧

ADORATIONS

THE LOVE STAR–*"The Secret"*

Love Star, Love Star, Love Star bright,
Love Star, Love Star, blaze through us Thy Might;
Love Star, Love Star, our own Hearts' Light!
Love Star, Love Star, enfold us tonight.

THE GRAIL

We, as One, offer ourselves as a Grail, a Crystal Cup of Thy Mighty Presence, O "Beloved I AM"! Keep It filled full to overflowing with Thy Glorious Life! Pour out through us Thy Mighty Love and Light, letting It flow forth as an ocean of Thy Blazing Essence, raising all into Thy Limitless Perfection forever.

ENFOLDED

I wear pure golden sandals
With ribbons of Light,
A crown made of Sun Rays,
A cloak of God's Might.
I carry a Scepter,
My Focus of Power;
I pour forth the Pure Christ
Each moment, each hour.

Note: We offer the following poem in Love and Adoration to our Beloved Ascended Master Saint Germain, for whom we call forth the Infinite Eternal Light and Love from the "Mighty I AM Presence," to bless Him with Its Mightiest Eternal Victory for the wonderful Gift of Himself to the Children of Light, that they, too, may manifest the same Perfection and Freedom which He is.

THE ASCENDED MASTER, SAINT GERMAIN

O Blest Saint Germain, Dear,
  Thou Holy Great One,
We love Thee and bless Thee,
  Thou God from the Sun.

We feel Thee and see Thee,
The Work Thou hast done,
For the Cup Thou dost carry
O'erflows from the "ONE."

We praise Thee and greet Thee,
Thou Great Lord of Light,
And raise now the Scepter
To Thy glorious Height.

We wield all Love's Power,
Love's Wisdom and Might;
Blaze through us forever
Thy Flame, Dazzling Bright.

Let all my Love flow back to Thee,
Thou Holy, Great God Flame of me!
Expand Thy Light and set me Free,
Let me Thyself forever *Be!*

✧

✧

Thou Adorable Supreme "I AM"! expand, expand, and again expand Thy Light in Eternal Glory through me.

"Beloved I AM Presence"! I offer my service to Thee in the capacity for which I am best fitted.

O "Mighty I AM Presence"! I love Thee, I bless Thee for the joy of Thy Glorious Light that lifts me beyond my outer self.

✧

You have the Opulence of the Universe to draw from!

✧✧✧

INVOCATIONS

THE LOVE STAR–*"The Call"*

O Love Star! we call Thee,
  Thou Jewel from the Sun,
O Heart of Creation,
  Thou Glorious One!
Come now in Thy Splendor,
  Flash forth Thy Great Flame,
Burst all bonds asunder,
  Speak forth the Great Name!
Declare now Thy Victory
  And set this Earth Free;
Reveal Thy Dominion,
  Thyself let all see.
From Thy Blazing Altar
  Light's Greeting first came,
The Voice of God's Presence,
  Almighty, "I AM"!

✧
✧
✧

Open, O Thou World-sustaining Sun, the entrance unto Truth! Hidden by the bars of Dazzling Light, soften the Radiation of Thy Illuminating Splendor, that we may behold Thy True Being. From the unreal lead us on to the Real, and unveil the human creation of the physical world, that we may know the Victory of the Ascension.

✧

My "Mighty I AM Presence"! Let me hear Thee and see Thee and feel Thee, and let me hold Thy Hand. Come! walk with me and talk with me. Oh, let me understand, know and remember all Reality. Let me forget all unreality and know myself as Thee and Thyself in me, as all of God's Great Blazing Light, for all Eternity.

RAISE US!

Raise us! Raise us! Raise us!
O Great "I AM" to Thee.
Raise us! Raise us! Raise us!
And set us ever Free.
Raise us! Raise us! Raise us!
To Thy Great Heights Divine.
Raise us! Raise us! Raise us!
We are forever Thine.

"Mighty I AM Presence"! project into this condition Thy Mighty Ascended Master Miracle-working Lightning of Divine Love. Blast everything human, its cause and effect into annihilation forever, and see that only Thy Miracles of Eternal Peace, Love, Harmony, Illumination, Protection and Perfection ever come out of it to all concerned.

"Mighty I AM Presence"! come forth this instant and charge this entire condition (person, place or thing) with the Fullness of Thyself! Project into it Thy Miracle-working Lightning of Divine Love and compel only Ascended Master Miracles of Perfection to come out of it to everyone; and keep them eternally sustained and ever expanding.

"Mighty I AM Presence"! come through me! Do this thing perfectly! and see that I expand Thy Perfection, forever.

"Mighty I AM Presence"! take me into your Heart tonight while my body sleeps! Instruct me in the fullness of the Ascended Masters' Understanding of the "I AM Presence"! See that I bring back that Instruction clearly into all my outer activity when I awaken in the morning, and make me always express Thy Full Perfection forever.

"Mighty I AM Presence"! come forth in the Full Dominion of the combined Ascended Host, and make every educational activity a crystal clear channel through which the Ascended Masters can always work for the Purity, Protection and Perfection of the Youth of America and the world.

"Mighty I AM Presence"! come forth and project Thy Lightning of Divine Love in Its most powerful, dynamic Activity into every educational channel on earth! Annihilate forever all teaching that is not the fullness of the Ascended Masters' Truth and Consciousness! Fill the minds and hearts of all mankind with the "Light of God that never fails," compelling Perfection to come forth everywhere to bless all forever with the "Power of a Thousand Suns."

"Mighty I AM Presence"! descend into this place! Do Thy Perfect Work and hold Thy Full Dominion here forever.

✧

"Mighty I AM Presence"! sweep into this_______! Annihilate everything human within it! Release Thy Mighty Power! Compel a Mighty Miracle of Perfection to come out of it to all concerned, and keep it forever sustained by Thy Mighty Presence which "I AM."

"Mighty I AM Presence"! charge me and my world with the Violet Consuming Flame of Divine Love which consumes all that is undesirable; and keep me clothed forever with Thy Almighty Perfection.

"Mighty I AM Presence"! take out of me all doubt and fear, and charge me with Thy Eternal Love, Courage, Strength, Protection, and ever-expanding Perfection.

"Mighty I AM Presence"! sweep in here, make all things new instantly and hold Thy Full Dominion forever!

"Mighty I AM Presence"! raise everything in my being and world into the Heart of Thy Secret Love Star and see that I abide in Thy Great Peace and Self-control forever.

"Mighty I AM Presence"! lock me within Thy Perfect Self-control and hold me there forever.

The "Mighty I AM Presence" is always the only Governing Intelligence here.

"Mighty I AM Presence"! turn me from that human experience! Take it into oblivion and make me forget it forever!

"Mighty I AM Presence"! seize possession and control of my attention! Keep it upon Thee and Thy Perfection forever, and do not let it ever wander again.

"Mighty I AM Presence"! see that I never miss or disobey a Direction from Thee! See that I do only that which expands Thy Perfection everywhere forever.

"Mighty I AM Presence"! make and keep me infinitely sensitive to Thee and Thy Perfection, forever in the Heart of Thy Love, and absolutely nonrecordant to everything else.

"Mighty I AM Presence"! take this doubt out of me! Make me see, feel and BE the fullness of this Truth and Thy Perfection forever!

"Mighty I AM Presence"! protect forever every Student in this Group, and all under this Radiation, and hold each one steady in his effort to reach Perfection.

"Mighty I AM Presence"! take me to the Golden Temple of Light tonight while my body sleeps! Charge my being and world with Its Light, Energy and Perfection, and see that I bring back Its Full Perfection into my physical body and outer activity when I awaken.

"Mighty I AM Presence"! put me into my Perfect Work now, and make me do it perfectly.

"Mighty I AM Presence"! show me what You want me to do now, and make me do it perfectly.

"Mighty I AM Presence"! consume in me and my world all doubt, fear, jealousy, pride, resentment, irritation, criticism, condemnation and judgment, their cause and effect, replacing them by the Fullness of the Perfection which Thou art, keeping It Self-sustained in the ever expanding Light of Thy Glorious Presence.

"Mighty I AM Presence"! shatter and consume forever this discordant condition in and with ____________________________! Annihilate its cause and effect throughout the Earth forever, and see that it never touches our lives or world again.

"Mighty I AM Presence"! seize possession of that (or this) mind and body! Enter in! Hold Your Dominion; and compel the attention to be anchored forever upon Thee and Thy Eternal Perfection.

"Mighty I AM Presence"! seize possession of these eyes! Look through them perfectly! Make them see and visualize only Perfection, forever Self-sustained.

"Mighty I AM Presence"! take possession of and command me forever; see that nothing ever gets my attention again but Thee and Thy Perfection.

"Mighty I AM Presence"! take possession of my mind, body, being and world forever! Lock them against the recognition of all human creation! Fasten my attention entirely upon Thee and Thy Perfection! Cut me free forever from the magnetic pull of Earth, the things of Earth and all human creation. Fill me with Thyself, Thy Full Ascended Master Consciousness and Mastery and hold Thy Full Eternal Dominion.

✧

"Mighty I AM Presence"! take complete control of my Being, world, and activity! and see that I make my Ascension in this embodiment; for "I AM" the Resurrection and the Life! "I AM" the Ascension in the Light!

Use once an hour:

"Mighty I AM Presence"! come forth, charge my being and world with the Light and Love from the Secret Love Star, and keep It eternally sustained.

"Mighty I AM Presence"! I here, now, and forever give You all Power! I give You all Obedience! Take charge of this mind and body! Prepare it to become the Ascended Master and see that I make my Ascension now.

"Mighty I AM Presence"! charge me with the Ascended Masters' Feeling and Victory of the Ascension.

"Mighty I AM Presence"! see that I make my Ascension now!

"Mighty I AM Presence"! take me into Your Heart and reveal to me and through me the Fullness of Thyself, instantly, infinitely, and eternally manifest.

"Mighty I AM Intelligence"! bring this Eternal Victory of Light and Love to pass now, in all Thy Blazing Glory.

"Mighty I AM Presence"! lock my mind and feeling forever against everything but Thy full "Presence" and Its Perfect Activity, instantly and eternally manifest.

"Mighty I AM Presence"! descend into this Thy mind and body. Take full Conscious Control this instant of all its activities; and hold Thy Dominion and Victory here forever!

"Mighty I AM Presence"! draw me within the most Blazing Light of Your Heart, and seal me there forever, that only Your Fullest Perfection may express.

"Mighty I AM Presence"! come forth! Charge my being and world with that Light and Love as of a thousand suns, and crowd my path with showers and showers of Blessings and Ascended Master Miracles and Victories of Light, forever.

Come forth, "Mighty I AM Presence"! Manifest Thy Mighty Miracles of Perfection instantly; and see that only the greatest, most transcendent good comes out of this occurrence forever.

For mistakes in others:

"Mighty I AM Presence"! forgive them for they know not what they do; and do Thou, my own God Flame, see that I do not do it too.

"Mighty I AM Presence"! forgive my mistakes! Come forth in Thy Infinite Power, and transmute that energy into a Mighty Ascended Master Miracle of Perfection made manifest today.

"Mighty I AM Presence"! henceforth, You are the Doer! Come forth and take command here forever!

"Mighty I AM Presence"! take complete possession of my attention and my feelings, and fill them entirely with Thyself.

"Mighty I AM Presence"! come forth and manifest Thy Supreme Authority of Divine Love in my being and world forever.

"Mighty I AM Presence"! show me Your Perfect Channel for this activity. Open it to me through Divine Love, and put me to work within it at once, producing Your Perfection forever.

Make me a new Heart, O "Mighty I AM Presence," and let me feel the Fullness of Thyself within me.

"Mighty I AM Presence"! charge me full to overflowing forever with:

Inexhaustible Strength and Energy,
Indestructible Health,
Invincible Protection,
Irresistible Divine Love,
Inescapable Prosperity,
Ascended Master Consciousness,
Illumination,
Freedom, and
Use of Thy Full Power instantly and eternally manifest.

For business dealings:

"Mighty I AM Presence"! I want the Perfection of Your World brought into mine! Take command here and produce Your Victory forever!

"Mighty I AM Presence"! You are the only Presence, Power, and Intelligence acting in my business. Protect and take it forward to Your Complete Success and Perfection, forever Self-sustained in Blazing, Glorious Light, manifesting Mighty Miracles of Perfection, now.

"Mighty I AM Presence"! charge my entire mind and body with Thy Ascended Master Consciousness and keep It eternally sustained.

"Mighty I AM Presence"! see that the flesh of this body never again records any human quality; and keep it forever filled only with Thyself, and express Thy Glorious Perfection.

"Mighty I AM Presence"! these are Your hands. Pour forth through them always Thy Healing Miracles and Full Perfection.

"Mighty I AM Presence"! this is Your brain; these are Your hands; play with Your Mighty Perfection and produce Your Mighty Glory and Music of the Spheres!

"Mighty I AM Presence"! illumine this for me and tell me Your Full Truth concerning it.

"Mighty I AM Presence"! make me fully comprehend this which I wish to know and understand right now.

Come forth, Thou "Mighty I AM Presence"! and blaze through me now and forever "The Light of God That Never Fails."

"Mighty I AM Presence"! take me deep within the Heart of the Great Central Sun! Charge my consciousness with that Light! Teach me the Full Ascended Masters' Knowledge of the Flame; and see that I awaken with that Knowledge in my brain consciousness.

"Mighty I AM Presence"! I call unto Thee as never before! Answer Thou me with the Full Freedom of Thyself.

"Mighty I AM Presence"! put me in my own right harmonious place and sustain me there.

"Mighty I AM Presence"! I thank Thee for all the money that comes into my hands and use or that touches my world! I accept it as Thy Messenger of Love and Balance! Charge it with Thy Purity, Love and Blessing without limit; and see that it brings only Thy Freedom and Perfection everywhere in the world.

"Mighty I AM Presence"! move everywhere before me today, and do all for me and through me perfectly!

"Mighty I AM Presence"! protect me from the human suggestions of the outer world, that I may go forth only accepting Thy Mighty Self and Thy Perfection forever.

"Mighty I AM Presence"! surround America forever by Thy Circle of the Ascended Masters' Consuming Flame of Divine Love, which never admits anything unlike Thee or Thy Perfection.

"Mighty I AM Presence" and Mighty Ascended Masters! come forth in all outer activity! Seize control of America, the government, her people, and her resources! Hold them forever in the Heart of Thy Perfection; and bless all with Thy Happiness and Transcendent Light.

"Mighty I AM Presence"! come into this condition and solve it perfectly.

Do not use your energy to condemn politicians, but say many times a day for America:

In the Name of the "Mighty I AM Presence," I call the Light and Love of the Ascended Masters into the White House, into the National Capital, into every State in the Union, into the Hearts and minds of all politicians to produce Perfection NOW; and bring everything into Light's Victory of Divine Love.

In the Name of the "Mighty I AM Presence," I charge the minds and feelings of everybody in America with Saint Germain's Ascended Master Consciousness and Perfection. God bless, illumine, perfect and set them Free in the Service of the Light forever!

"Mighty I AM Presence"! shatter and consume all activity of the sinister force in America, its cause and effect, replacing it forever by the Eternal Perfection of the Ascended Masters' "Light of God That Never Fails."

Mighty Ascended Masters and Great Legions of Light! fill America with that Light, Love, Protection and Power as of a thousand suns, and keep Her forever Invincible to all but Thy Mighty Perfection.

✧ ✧ ✧

"Mighty I AM Presence"! You are the Power! You are the Intelligence acting here! Come forth and manage this outer activity now and forever with Ascended Master Management.

"Mighty I AM Presence"! come forth and annihilate this discordant action, its cause and effect, and put Thy Divine Perfection in its place forever.

"Mighty I AM Presence"! seize that energy! Requalify it by Your Divine Love and Perfection; and anchor it in my world, maintaining Ascended Master Protection and Perfection for me forever.

"Mighty I AM Presence"! either silence these discordant people, or put them where they belong; and bless them by Thy Power of Divine Love!

"Mighty I AM Presence"! come forth and manage this thing! Seize my attention and my feelings and hold them upon Thee forever!

"Mighty I AM Presence"! qualify every thought and feeling about this with the Ascended Masters' Accomplishment, Victory and Perfection.

My "Mighty I AM Presence"! Thou art my way, my protection, my defense and my deliverance from all disturbing conditions, and the instantaneous annihilation of their cause! Thou, my God-Victorious "Presence," come forth and manifest with Full Power through this mind and body forever.

Raise your hands to the "Mighty I AM Presence" and say:
"Mighty I AM Presence," come forth here! Silence that human nonsense, mentally and physically, forever.

"Mighty I AM Presence"! come into my mind and body this day! Manage me and hold Thy Supreme Dominion, forever.

"Mighty I AM Presence"! come forth! Right this condition and seal it in Thy Heart forever!

"Mighty I AM Presence"! produce Your Divine Love here and sustain It forever.

I call my "Mighty I AM Presence" and Saint Germain's Ascended Master Consciousness to come forth and solve this ____________ for me forever!

"Mighty I AM Presence"! come forth! Govern and solve this situation harmoniously forever.

"Mighty I AM Presence"! shut the door of my being and world forever against all human creation, and instantly annihilate all that attempts to open it.

"Mighty I AM Presence"! take care of my human creation, and see that I make the Ascension now, as quickly as possible.

"Mighty I AM Presence"! release Your Love and Light as of a Thousand Suns and maintain Your Perfection here forever!

"Mighty I AM Presence"! come forth! Charge my being and world every second of this day and forever with Ascended Master Perfection, instantly and eternally manifest.

"Mighty I AM Presence"! sweep my intellect clear from everything but Thee and Thy Perfection, and keep it so forever.

"Mighty I AM Presence"! charge my mind and body with Your Mighty Perfection forever.

"Mighty I AM Presence"! lock my mind and feelings forever against everything but Thy Full Perfection and Its Eternal Activity.

____*(name)*____ I, the "Mighty I AM Presence," speak to Thee: Awaken Thou! into the Perfection of Life!

"Mighty I AM Presence"! project Your Divine Love through me today, and forever pour out Your Full Dominion.

"Mighty I AM Presence"! command Divine Love to take full command of all my activity, and bring everything into Divine Order through Divine Love!

"Mighty I AM Presence"! charge me so full of Divine Love that every person, place, condition and thing I contact becomes instantly harmonious and obedient to Thee and Thy Perfection; and hold Thy Full Dominion forever.

Make me a new Heart, O "Mighty I AM Presence"! and keep the feeling of Thy Presence, Thy Light, Love and Victory within me forever.

"Mighty I AM Presence"! show me the Full Ascended Master Knowledge of everything concerning the Seven Mighty Elohim.

"Mighty I AM Presence"! make me Thy Supreme In-breathing and Outpouring of the Love from the Great Central Sun, forever.

"Mighty I AM Presence"! charge me with all the Perfection there is, everywhere present, visible and invisible; and keep It eternally sustained.

"Mighty I AM Presence"! take me to the Great Central Sun, and charge my brain, body and world with such tremendous Divine Love, Wisdom and

Power that It sweeps everything else before It; and make me express Thy Full Dominion.

"Mighty I AM Presence"! make me always Your most dynamic Action of Divine Love in Full Ascended Master Dominion through this brain and body, forever Self-sustained.

"Mighty I AM Presence"! raise the Liquid Light in my body. Take It back into Thyself, and produce Perfection in me forever!

"Mighty I AM Presence"! charge my body with Thy Light, until my face becomes Radiant and Self-luminous.

"Mighty I AM Presence"! seize possession of these eyes. Look through them perfectly, and see that they visualize only Perfection, forever Self-sustained!

"Mighty I AM Presence"! I call unto Thee! Answer Thou me! Blaze through my being and world forever Thy Full Dominion! Bring everything into Divine Order through Divine Love instantly, and keep it forever Self-sustained. Take complete control of my being and world! Manage my every activity with Ascended Master Management and compel all to manifest Thy Perfection, forever Self-sustained.

"Mighty I AM Presence"! charge me so full of Divine Love that every person, place, condition and thing I contact becomes instantly Harmonious and Obedient to the "I AM Presence."

"Mighty I AM Presence"! qualify all with Thy Perfection; and charge this Work with Saint Germain's Complete Ascended Master Consciousness, Protection and Perfection forever. I call unto Thee to come forth in the Fullness of Thy Power, and produce limitless Miracles and Victories of Thy Light forever.

"Mighty I AM Presence"! take charge of my attention! Anchor it into the Heart of Your Light and keep it there eternally.

✧

"Mighty I AM Presence"! show me Your Way. It seems to be my duty to do this thing; so show me Your Way.

"Mighty I AM Presence"! come forth! Illumine this thing for me and show me the Ascended Master Way.

"Mighty I AM Presence"! lock me in Thy Eternal, Perfect, Self-control that always consumes all human qualities and habits. This instant and forevermore manage all my activities and work, with Ascended Master Perfection. Release into my hands and outer use all Thy stored-up Treasures! Keep all forever Self-sustained through Thy Divine Love and express the Fullness of Thy Victory.

"Mighty I AM Presence"! take me within Thyself, instruct me, and cause me to retain the Full Memory of these Inner Instructions.

"Mighty I AM Presence"! come forth! Lock my being and world forever against all human creation! Keep my attention anchored upon the Ascended Master Consciousness and Perfection of the "I AM," the "Light of God That Never Fails."

"Mighty I AM Presence"! God in me, is my certain Victory, and I cannot fail!

"Mighty I AM Presence"! clothe me in the Ascended Masters' Consciousness of Divine Love forever!

"Mighty I AM Presence"! take me into Your Ascended Master Body and teach me the use of the Light Rays, that Thy Perfection may set me Free and reign forever upon Earth.

"Mighty I AM Presence"! charge my aura with instantaneous Healing to everybody that comes into my presence, and set all free in the Service of the Light.

"Mighty I AM Presence"! Stand guard and prevent any disembodied individual from coming into my aura at any time! Let nothing touch my consciousness but the Ascended Masters and the Angelic Host!

"Mighty, Majestic, Supreme I AM Presence"! in Thy great calm, serene Dominion I rest, yielding not to any human thing.

"Mighty I AM Presence"! charge me always with Your Mightiest, Dynamic Action of Divine Love, in

Full Ascended Master Dominion through this brain and body, forever Self-sustained.

"Mighty I AM Presence"! come forth and charge this house (home or activity) with the combined Love, Peace and Protection of the Ascended Host, and hold It there forever.

"Mighty I AM Presence"! see that this home, this environment, and all connected with it are governed harmoniously, and that all who enter manifest only the Ascended Master Activity.

"Mighty I AM Presence"! I wash my hands of all things human forever!

"Mighty I AM Presence"! insulate my mind, body, being and world forever from all human creation.

At least three times a day, stand on the floor with hands upraised and say:

"Mighty I AM Presence"! fill me with Your Love, Power and Perfect Intelligent Direction.

If confused, simply say:

"Mighty I AM Presence"! Light! Light! Light! Let there be more Light, the "Light of God That Never Fails"!

All activity in schools and colleges:

"Mighty I AM Presence"! blaze Thy Violet Lightning of Divine Love through all educational channels! Annihilate all wrong teaching of every kind, and its cause and effect throughout the Earth! Take possession of the brains and bodies of all students! Produce Thy Purity, Thy Perfection, Thy Protection! Illumine all by the Light of Thy Truth and keep It forever Self-sustained in the Eternal Glory and Victory of Thy Love.

"Mighty I AM Presence"! give me the time to do this thing (loving Thee), and make me do it in that time.

"Mighty I AM Presence"! give me this Perfect __________ (thing or condition) through Divine Love.

Visualize America as a Great Heart of Golden Flame, the outer Radiance violet surrounded by a Wall of Steely White Light. Make the Call:

Mighty Divine Director and Legions of Light! Fill America with that Light, Love, Protection, and Power as of a Thousand Suns that never fail, and keep Her forever Invincible to all but Thy Mighty Perfection.

"Mighty I AM Presence"! awaken all mankind! open all channels! and see that everyone accepts the Fullness of Thy Mighty "Presence" now, and receives Thy Eternal Freedom.

"Mighty I AM Presence"! make me feel Thy Rays of Divine Love every minute.

"Mighty I AM Presence"! I thank You for Your Life, Your Energy, and all You are constantly giving to me!

"Mighty I AM Presence"! raise and use all my Life Energy in Thy Limitless Intelligent Action forever.

"Mighty I AM Presence"! come into my mind and body this day and manage me forever!

If you want Freedom, you must give it first.

✧✧✧

AFFIRMATIONS

THE LOVE STAR–*"The Presence"*

The Love Star, His "Presence"!
All silent, serene,
In Glory transcendent
While blessing the scene;
Stands radiant with Power
Its Rays pulsing bright;
Chaste ribbons of silver
Adorning the night.
Caressing, encircling,
Enfolding the sod;
Light! tying the Earth to the
Feet of her God.
The Master Christ Presence
Incarnate in man,
The Source of all Freedom,
The Blest Word, "I AM"!

INVOCATION TO THE FLAME

"I AM"! the Eternal Flame of Life, a White-Fire Being from the Heart of God! In-breathing the Great Love Breath of the Almighty, I dwell within my Golden Ray from the Great Central Sun! Crowned with the Diamond Rays of Attainment, I abide upon my Sacred Lotus Throne of Light, letting my Love flow out unto all creation! "I AM" a Sun in the Palace of Infinite Light! My world, the Altar of Infinite Space! My Radiance, the Peace of the Great Solar Quiet! "I AM" the Undying Flame of Life everywhere, the Great Eternal Joy and Glory and Perfection of existence. "I AM"! "I AM"! "I AM"! Three times three "I AM"!

"I AM"! Elohim, Elohim, Elohim,
Elohim, Elohim, Elohim, Elohim!
Seven times seven "I AM," ELOHIM!

✦

Note: Students affirm:

"I AM"! the Ascended Masters' Eternal Acceptance of this.

"I AM"! always the Majestic Presence and Miracle-working Power of Divine Love that transcends every human concept; blazing through me and to me forever all the Perfection from within Its Heart, with the Power of a Thousand Suns. 

"I AM"! the Eternal Ceaseless Flow of the Blazing Light from my "I AM Presence" through my mind and body.

"I AM"! forever God-commanded.

Make your outer mind continually acknowledge:

"I AM"! through the veil now!

"I AM"! the Ascended Master Presence I desire to be, and "I AM"! the Ascended Master Consciousness of this Victory. *(Then be sure the personality does not think, say, feel, see, hear, or do anything unlike the Perfection of the Ascended Masters.)*

"I AM" the "Presence" raising the atomic structure of this body to the Ascended Masters' full Illumination and Liberation.

"I AM"! the Mighty Flame of Life, raising all in my being and world into the Diamond Heart, and holding it there forever.

"I AM"! the Ascended Master Consciousness everywhere that does all things perfectly today.

"I AM"! the Ascended Master Control of all my energy forever.

"I AM"! Christ! God in Action! The "Light of God that never fails," in the Fullness of Its Eternal Victory and Dominion.

"I AM" the "Presence" qualifying all my feeling with the Full Perfection and Expansion of the Ascended Master Consciousness.

"I AM"! the Ascended Master Control of that habit in you, _____.

"I AM"! the Pure Electronic Body of Light, illumining every person, place, condition and thing wherever I am or pass by, and all my thought rests upon.

"I AM"! the positive, rich, full, clear, perfect, loving Voice of the Ascended Masters, and I speak only as They speak, now and forever.

"I AM"! all the vigor and resilience of Eternal Youth and Beauty, and all the Wisdom, Strength, Courage, Power and Self-control of my "I AM Presence," expressing only Full Ascended Master Perfection forever.

To help others:

Here pal: "I AM"! the Strength in you that conquers that.

Here pal: "I AM"! a mountain of Light, Love and Strength in you that never fails.

"I AM"! always the Limitless Peace of the Eternal.

"The Light of God never fails" and "I AM"! that Light–God in Action–for God in me is always my certain Eternal Victory.

"I AM"! the instant, the hour and the day of Fulfillment.

"I AM" the "Presence" qualifying this with a Mountain of Light that casts no shadow, and in which are all good things.

Whenever you think of what you want, say:

"I AM" the "Presence" qualifying every thought and feeling about this with the Ascended Masters' Accomplishment and Victory.

I do know the Ascended Master Thing to do in this situation, and "I AM" the "Presence" doing it now, instantly and eternally victorious.

To human creation say:

No! Now you get out! The "Mighty I AM Presence" is in control here and I know it!

Know:

The "Mighty I AM Presence" is in and all about this person, place, condition or thing, and only God in action acts back to me.

Say to all disturbing persons, conditions or human creation:

"I AM" the "Presence" commanding Silence! Peace! and Obedience! to the "Mighty I AM Presence" forever.

"Mighty, Majestic, Supreme I AM Presence"! in Thy Great, Calm, Serene Dominion I rest forever, yielding not to any human thing.

"I AM" the "Presence" that never doubts, fears, questions, nor is uncertain concerning the instantaneous Fulfillment of my every Call to the "Mighty I AM Presence."

"I AM"! the Ascended Masters' Eternal Divine Memory.

"I AM"! the Guard, Self-sustained forever, that gives out only Truth and Perfection.

"I AM" the "Presence" of Divine Love and Intelligence, acting in all these Classes, and the Ascended Masters' Victory of Light eternally sustained.

I awake! I arise! I shine! for my Light is come! And the Glory of the "Mighty I AM Presence" is blazing and Invincible within me!

"I AM"! the Ascended Master Management of everything in my world forever.

"I AM"! always the Ascended Masters' Revelation, Acceptance and Use of all the Powers of the Being which "I AM."

"I AM"! always the unyielding, joyous Determination of the "Great I AM" releasing Perfection everywhere.

"I AM" the "Presence" of the Great Silence!

"I AM" the "Presence," Love, and Power in you that conquers that.

"I AM"! now the Full Confidence of the "Mighty I AM Presence" forever.

"I AM"! the feeling of the Great "I AM."

"I AM" the "Presence" that forgives and forgets all human mistakes forever and replaces them with the Infinite "I AM" Perfection, eternally sustained, in Blazing Glory and ever-expanding.

I do know the Ascended Master thing to do every second, every day, and I do it always.

There is no personality in my world today! There is only God in Action, the "Mighty I AM Presence."

"I AM" sealed forever in the Peace, Protection, Security, Love, Wisdom, Power, Supply and Freedom of the "Light of God that never fails."

"I AM"! the Almightiness of the Great Silence.

"I AM"! the Ascended Master Consciousness and ever-present Victory of all I desire to do forever.

Before going to sleep:

Through the Presence, Power and Intelligence which "I AM," I go forth while my body sleeps, feeling and experiencing the Fullness of myself as the Infinite "I AM Presence," and when my body awakens, charging it full to overflowing with the feeling of that "Presence."

"I AM"! the Freedom of the Great "I AM."

"I AM"! eternally God-controlled every moment, every day, in everything, and every way.

Because "I AM" Thee and Thou art me, "I AM" Protected, Illumined, Supplied and Free!

What is that to me? I follow Thee, Thou Infinite "Almighty I AM Presence" forever!

Peace! Peace! Peace! Be still! "I AM"! Perfect Obedience to my Inner Will.

My eyes are the Eyes of the "Mighty I AM Presence." I see all things and through all things perfectly, and I see Perfection everywhere.

My ears are the Ears of the "Mighty I AM Presence." I listen only to the Voice of my "I AM Presence," accept only Its Truth, and hear only the Music of the Spheres perfectly forever.

The Light of the "I AM" is Mighty and does prevail, and I feel Its Victorious, Majestic Presence controlling at all times within me.

"I AM"! the Pure, Crystal Clear Mind of God the "Mighty I AM Presence" in that *(or this)* brain and body, maintaining Ascended Master Consciousness and Dominion there forever!

"I AM"! the Pure Sight of God, the "Mighty I AM Presence," and I see Perfection everywhere.

"I AM" the "Presence" that does not take on suggestions from anybody or anything about me, but God! Good!

"I AM" the "Presence" that can and does clear all human concepts of mankind permanently everywhere I go, because "I AM"! God in Action.

"I AM" the "Presence" refusing all human interference forever with this Work and Light of the "I AM Presence" in ourselves, the Students, or anything under this Radiation, in America and the world.

"I AM"! always the Miracle-working Presence in everything I desire to have done.

"I AM"! always Perfect Poise that controls everything instantly and harmoniously through Divine Love.

"I AM" the "Presence" that is always proof against any and every sudden disturbance forever.

"I AM" the "Presence" who is never disturbed or off guard.

Acknowledge often:

"I AM" the "Presence," commanding a Gigantic Ascended Miracle of Perfection to come out of every situation through Divine Love.

"I AM" the Pure Mind of God, the "Mighty I AM Presence" forever!

"I AM"! the Pure Love of God, the "Mighty I AM Presence"!

"I AM"! the Pure Feeling of God, the "Mighty I AM Presence"!

"I AM"! the Pure Speech of God, the "Mighty I AM Presence"!

"I AM"! the Pure Sight of God, the "Mighty I AM Presence"!

"I AM"! the Pure Hearing of God, the "Mighty I AM Presence"! Forever, forever, and forever.

✧

"I AM"! the Resurrection, the Life, the Health, and the Light of my body, made manifest in and through my flesh today!

"I AM"! LIGHT, LIGHT, LIGHT! ALL LIGHT! This is the Master Record upon which humanity was modeled in the beginning, the Image and Likeness of God, the "Mighty I AM Presence."

"I AM"! the positive, poised, peaceful, loving control of this whole situation forever.

"I AM" the Conquering "Presence." I command this "Presence" to take control of all my affairs and produce Perfection always.

"I AM" the Controlling, Harmonizing "Presence" everywhere I move and of everything to which my thought is directed, bringing all into Divine Order through Divine Love.

"I AM"! come within the Stillness of Thy Heart! my "Mighty Majestic I AM Presence"! Keep me sealed in It forever, that only Thy Full Perfection shall always express.

"I AM"! the Ascended Master Control and Qualification of all the energy of my being and world, forever manifest in Full Power with the speed of thought.

I go forth this day with the tread of a Mighty Conqueror, Lord of Life and Victor over death and hell, Glorious, Supreme in the Great God Flame of Life, and "I AM"! Free! Forever Free!

"I AM"! the Ascended Master Payment of this (of every) bill or obligation, instantly and eternally manifest through Divine Love.

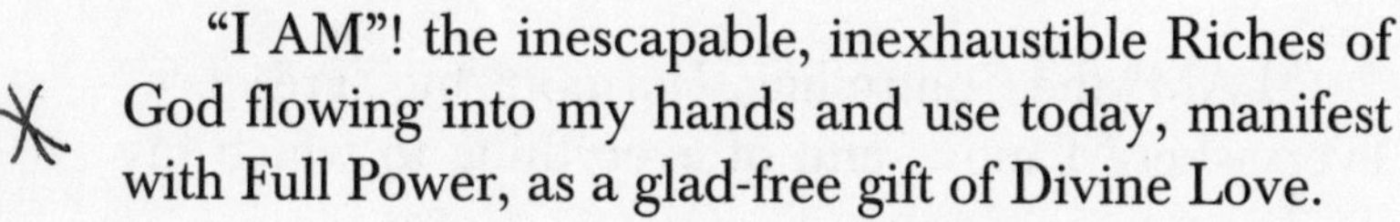

"I AM"! the inescapable, inexhaustible Riches of God flowing into my hands and use today, manifest with Full Power, as a glad-free gift of Divine Love.

I refuse everything but the Fullness of God's Supply to me, NOW!

"I AM"! the Ascended Masters' Fulfillment of the Divine Law, the Law of Love, concerning this money in the handling of these ____________.

✧ ✧ ✧

The Love that "I AM" greets the Love in you, and the God Flame of "I AM" comes instantly through and releases Its Perfection, forever.

"I AM"! the Fire Breath of Divine Love from the Great Secret Love Star.

"I AM" the "Presence" charging my being and world forever with the Pure Power and Feeling of the Flame of Divine Love from the Lords of the Flame from Venus, and keeping It forever manifest in Supreme Victory.

"I AM" the Majesty of Divine Love and the Ascended Master Victory in my being and world, forever Self-sustained.

"I AM" here and "I AM" there! "I AM"! Divine Love and Blessing everywhere.

O Masters of the Diamond Heart!
I call now unto Thee!
Pour out Thy Flame forevermore,
Thy Great Love Power through me.

"I AM" the Heartbeat of Divine Love! the Great Secret Love Breath of the "Mighty I AM Presence."

"I AM" always the Majestic Power of Pure Love that transcends every human concept, and opens the Door to me to the Light within Its Heart.

"I AM"! the Great Love Flame of the Almighty, manifest with Full Power through this, my mind and body forever.

I invoke the Full "I AM" Power and Activity of Divine Love in my being and world today and forever, manifest with the speed of thought.

Silence! Peace! and Obedience! to the "Mighty I AM Presence" forever!

"I AM" the "Presence" thinking through this mind and body forever.

"I AM" the "Presence" that nothing ever opposes.

"I AM" the "Presence" to whom there is no interference and no delay.

"I AM" the ever-present Ascended Master Protection in my being and world, that no human creation can ever break through.

"I AM"! the Ascended Masters' annihilation of this, and its cause and effect forever.

"I AM"! always the Master Presence and Eternal Victory of the "Light of God That Never Fails."

"I AM"! always surrounded by that Circle of Consuming Fire, which does not admit anything unlike the Christ, the Ascended Masters' Perfection.

Through the "Presence" which "I AM" this thing shall cease now and forever, and is replaced by Saint Germain's Perfection.

I do accept the Full Dominion of my "Mighty I AM Presence" in my being and world forever.

Remember again and again, that as you grow into the Full Acceptance of your "Mighty I AM Presence," your outer problems will disappear; for "I AM" the "Presence" dissolving all problems permanently. Then, visualize the Mantle of Invisibility enfolding you.

"I AM" the "Mighty Presence" on guard forever.

"I AM"! the Invincible Guard; established, sustained and maintained over my mind, my body, my home, my world and my affairs forever.

"I AM"! the Ascended Master Annihilation of all human creation in my mind, body and world, now and forever.

In the Name of the "Mighty I AM," which "I AM"! I silence, shatter, and consume this human creation and its cause forever.

When necessary to discuss some discordant condition, say:

"I AM" the "Presence" withdrawing all energy from

the words and feelings expressed, and I requalify it with Thy Purity and Love and hold it in my world, maintaining Ascended Master Protection and Perfection for me.

"I AM" the "Presence" refusing acceptance of this discordant outer thing. I shut my door and it stays out.

The "Mighty I AM Presence" is my Way, my Protection, my Defense and my Deliverance from every disturbing condition, and the Release of the Full Dominion of the Ascended Masters' Light, Love and Victory in all my activities now and forever.

"I AM"! the ever-present Ascended Master Protection, that no human creation can ever break through.

The Love that "I AM" greets the Love in you, and this Pure Liquid Light comes instantly through, and heals you forever.

"I AM"! the Ascended Master Release of this Perfect Activity, Precipitation, instantly manifest with Full Power and Ascended Master Protection.

"I AM"! the All-Knowing Mind of God! I do know the right solution of this problem, and I solve it now through Divine Love.

"I AM" the "Presence" and Power in my world this day that conquer every problem by the "Light and Love of God that never fail," and that hold Its Eternal Victory and Freedom.

I place all my problems within the Heart of the "Great I AM," and "I AM" at Peace in the "Light of God That Never Fails."

"I AM"! the Mighty Ascended Master Solution of this problem, now and forever.

"I AM"! the Ascended Masters' Instantaneous Solution and Miraculous Victory in this problem, and the feeling of God control fills me forever.

"I AM" the "Presence" and Power in you that conquers this problem, for "I AM" your Supreme Victory over this human nonsense.

"I AM"! the Supreme Victory over all human consciousness forever.

I now cast all this human creation, its cause and effect into the Sea of Consuming Fire and Eternal Forgetfulness, replacing it by the Presence and Eternal Perfection of the "Great I AM."

God, the "Mighty I AM Presence," is alive within me. I do not allow that "Glorious Being" to be silenced by the doubts and fears of my human self.

"I AM"! the Ascended Masters' Attainment of Divine Love forever.

"I AM"! a Mountain of Divine Love that brings all Miracles to pass instantly at my command forever.

"I AM"! the Love and the Strength in you that conquers, and the "I AM" is your Victory!

"I AM"! always the Love of the "Great I AM" forever.

"I AM"! the Ascended Masters' Freedom of Divine Love in Full Control at all times.

"I AM" the "Presence" and limitless Focus of such Divine Love in this _______ as has never been experienced before on Earth, and "I AM" the "Presence" keeping It forever Self-sustained in Full Power.

"I AM"! the All-controlling Presence of Divine Love at all times. "I AM" the Herculean Love of the "Mighty I AM Presence," controlling and acting in Full Ascended Master Consciousness through this mind and body forever.

The Love that "I AM" greets the Love in you, and this Miracle of "I AM" comes instantly through, and blesses you with Perfection forever, for in the Fullness of that Love is the Victory you desire.

Peace! Peace! Peace be still! "I AM" this Miracle of Love's Great Will.

"I AM" this Mighty Ascended Master Miracle performed today with the speed of thought, and made manifest with Full Power. I thank Thee, "Great I AM."

"I AM" the Presence of Divine Love blessing every atom into Peace and Perfection.

"I AM"! the Presence of Divine Love perfecting everything there.

"I AM"! the Supreme In-breathing and Outpouring of the Great Love Breath of the "Mighty I AM Presence" forever.

"I AM" the "Presence" entering into, revealing and charging all my outer activity with the Music of the Spheres, Instantaneous Healing, Ascended Master Precipitation, and the Eternal Dominion of Divine Love.

"I AM"! the Ascended Masters' Instantaneous Precipitation and visible Presence of everything I desire; and no human consciousness can interfere with It.

"I AM"! the combined Presence and Power of the Ascended Host, standing like a Wall of Light, instantly annihilating everything that attempts disturbance or interference with anybody or anything under this Radiation.

✧

Students are to feel this for each other:

"I AM" the "Presence" that loves you into your perfect Ascended Master Activity. "I AM" the

"Presence" that loves you into your conscious ability to do this.

"I AM"! the Ascended Master Consciousness of Boundless Divine Love flooding all everywhere.

"I AM"! the Great Love Flame of the Almighty, manifest with Full Power through this, my mind and body forever.

"I AM" sealed within the Love Flame from the Secret Heart of God. "I AM" the "Presence" sealing you in the Love Flame from the Secret Heart of God.

"I AM"! the Overflowing Presence of Divine Love ruling everywhere.

"I AM"! the Presence and Power of the Ascended Masters' Love here which never fails.

"I AM"! the Strength, Courage, and Power to move forward steadily through all experiences whatever they may be, and remain joyous and uplifted, feeling only the Peace and Harmony at all times of the Glorious Presence which "I AM"!

"I AM"! always enfolded in the Mantle of the Master Christ; therefore, I maintain my thoughts, feelings and words free from all criticism and judgment.

Illumination of body, mind and atmosphere:

"I AM" the "Presence" illumining this mind, body and room with the Blazing Light of the Ascended Master, and keeping It forever sustained in Full Power through Divine Love.

"I AM"! Jesus Christ's Ascended Master Consciousness of my attainment of the Ascension.

Use this often, for it stills the outer activity, so you become centered in the activity of Divine Love:

"I AM"! the Commanding Presence.

"I AM" Ascended! "I AM" Ascended! "I AM" Ascended! "I AM" Ascended! in the Mighty Strength of my dauntless "Mighty I AM Presence" which is forever unconquerable, unquenchable, unalterable in Its everlasting Perfection, Mastery, Victory, and Majesty expressed through this mind and body now, which is no longer human but Divine. All earthly activity shall bow before me, be silent, and obey the Christ in me forever in the Service of the Light.

The most permanent, Perfect Way to illumine the physical body is to take the consciousness that:

"I AM" expressing and radiating the brilliant LIGHT OF GOD, the "I AM Presence," in me, and illumining this body for me.

Say to the body:

"I AM" the "Presence" commanding you to be strong and take on the Beauty of Form and Expression of the "Mighty I AM Presence" forever.

For heart trouble say:

My breath is the great Love Breath from out the Great Central Sun. My Heart is God's Heart, the very center of Divine Love, and Its Light fills me now!

"I AM" the "Light of God that never fails" now made permanently manifest in my flesh as Self-luminosity.

"I AM" the cleansing process always active in my mind and body, consuming all imperfection and revealing the Purity "I AM."

"I AM" the Resurrection and Life of my business, my understanding and whatever I wish to center my attention upon.

"I AM" the Resurrection, the Life and the Health of my body made manifest in my flesh today.

Hands and feet:

These are God's Hands and Feet and I charge them with the Power, Perfection and Perfect Love of the "Mighty I AM Presence" forever.

"I AM"! the Mighty Electronic Energy flowing through, filling and renewing every cell of my mind and body, right now.

"I AM" the "Presence" breathing Perfection in and through this physical flesh body forever.

The "I AM Presence" governs this physical body completely and compels it into obedience.

"I AM" the "Presence" qualifying this mind and body with absolute Perfection, and refusing acceptance to anything else.

Whatever there is of imperfection in me must get out! I qualify everything in my being and world this day with Perfection, because "I AM" Perfection!

Contemplation:

"I AM" come within the stillness of Thy Heart, my "Mighty Majestic I AM Presence"! Keep me sealed in It forever, that only Thy full Perfection shall always express.

Whatever is under the whole heaven is mine to love and to bless forever, with the Perfection of the "Mighty I AM Presence."

"I AM" the "Presence" commanding the visible and tangible Presence of the Ascended Host with us now, in the physical octave. *(Go on! Accept this, and stick to it!)*

"I AM"! the Master within, governing and controlling all my thought processes in Full Christ Perfection, as I wish them to be.

"I AM" the "Presence" arranging my time in Perfect Divine Order.

"I AM" the "Presence" producing the perfect business I desire.

"I AM"! the Mighty Cosmic Light, Divine Justice and Protection acting in the minds and Hearts of individuals everywhere.

"I AM" always loving Obedience to the Light.

"I AM"! "I AM"! I know "I AM"! Free from this thing forever, no matter what it is.

"I AM"! the Ascended Master Consciousness Self-sustained that does not permit me to give out anything but that which is Perfect.

"I AM" no longer the "Babe of Christ," but the "Master Presence" grown to full stature, and I speak and command with authority.

"I AM"! the Law of Forgiveness and the Consuming Flame of the Ascended Masters, freeing me forever from all but the Perfection of the "I AM."

"I AM"! the Ascended Masters' Eternal, Complete and Unconditional Forgiveness and Forgetfulness of all human creation, past, present and future, and the replacement of it by the Full Perfection of the Ascended Masters forever.

"I AM" always proof against any sudden disturbance!

✧

"I AM"! Inexhaustible Energy!
"I AM"! Irresistible Divine Love!
"I AM"! Indestructible Health!
"I AM"! Inescapable Prosperity!
"I AM"! Invincible Protection!

"I AM"! the "Mighty Presence" on guard every second this day, instantly annihilating all that seeks to disturb, and holding my full God Dominion in this place forever.

"I AM" superior to discord; I can't afford to be bothered.

"I AM"! the Commanding Presence!
"I AM"! the Conquering Presence!
"I AM"! the Victorious Presence!
"I AM"! the Majestic Presence!
"I AM"! the Ascended Presence!

✧

"I AM"! the Presence of enough Love to release and reveal the Almightiness of the Great God-Self, "I AM"! forever.

"I AM"! the one Eternal, Self-sustained Life in action, ever expanding Perfection.

"I AM" the "Presence" producing abundance wherever I choose to use it, in the Service of Perfection! the Light.

In the Name of the "Mighty I AM Presence," the Ascended Masters and the "Light of God That Never Fails," all discordant activity within America shall cease, now and forever!

The "Presence" that "I AM" clothes these, my Beloved Ones, in their Eternal Transcendent Garments of Light.

The "Presence" that "I AM" clothes me now in my Eternal Transcendent Garment of Light.

O Blessed Flame of Divine Love, "I AM" Thy Pure Presence forever.

"I AM"! the All-Knowing, Dazzling, Fathomless Mind of God, the "Mighty I AM Presence"! Its

Almighty Intelligence, Its Boundless Knowledge, Its Limitless Wisdom, Its Infinite Inspiration, Its Eternal Truth, Its Full Illumination, Its Complete Perfection and Invincible Protection, releasing through me now Transcendent Ideas of Perfection from the Secret Heart of God, that have never come forth before anywhere in the Universe.

"I AM"! the Presence of Divine Love blessing everybody and everything in this business into Perfection, instantly and eternally manifest with Full Power.

"I AM"! every deal closed that brings Perfection to those buying these ________.

"I AM"! the Ascended Master Ease, Peace, Comfort, Purity, Control, and Conservation of all the Energy in my being and world forever.

Every day, speak to your body! Command it to be strong, receptive only to the Ascended Master Consciousness, to be a Perfect Expression of the Divine Presence of the "Mighty I AM," and to take on Its Beauty of form and expression:

"I AM" the "Light of God that never fails" now made permanently manifest in my flesh, as self-luminosity in Blazing Glory.

The "Mighty I AM Presence" is the only Healing Presence; and through It, I have the right to command all outer activity to be silent and obey my command.

"Choose ye this day whom ye shall serve."

To dismiss discord say:

'Tis a wave on the ocean of human emotion,
It's nothing, it's nothing at all;
It comes like a flicker
And goes away quicker
When I on my God-Self do call.
It is only a cloud
But I say aloud,
"I AM" the Sun! Don't you see?
I blaze the Light!
You fade from sight!
And all things now obey me.
(*Or:* The Light yields all things to me.)

People are bound because they bind others.

✧✧✧

SALUTATIONS

THE LOVE STAR–*"The All"*

The Love Star, the Flame Breath,
  The Great Heart in all,
Comes forth in Its Splendor
  To answer each Call;
Reveals now Its Vict'ry,
  In all Realms Its Light,
Clothes us in Its Glory
  And Radiance bright;
Let all then surrender
  Their might and their power,
Through loving Obedience
  Be raised now this hour.
Forevermore Master!
  Eternally free!
The Blest "I AM Presence,"
  The Great Cosmic Key.

THE GREAT COSMIC BEING, SURYA

Surya, Surya, Surya!
Thou Great Blessed God from the Sun!
Surya, Surya, Surya!
Blaze forth Thy Great Light–make all One!
Surya, Surya, Surya!
Make us like Thyself–all Divine!
Surya, Surya, Surya!
Come through! We are evermore Thine.

THE LORD, THE MAHA CHOHAN

Maha Chohan! Maha Chohan! Maha Chohan! raise us all into Thy dazzling Jesus Christ Illumination, that we may become that Blazing White Light that draws all mankind upward until they become that Great Light also.

✧

THE SILENT WATCHER

(Sung to the melody of *Absent* by Metcalf)

O Silent Watcher
  of Infinity!
Great Brooding Presence,
  All dwell within Thee;
Boundless Thy Love
  In earth, and sky, and sea;
O Silent Watcher,
  Thy Great God Self we see.

O Silent Watcher,
  Great God from the Sun!
I feel Thy Love,
  For Thou and I are One.
Shed forth Thy Light,
  Let all Thy Love now be;
O Silent Watcher,
  Through all Eternity.

O Silent Watcher,
  Blessed Self of me!
O Love Divine,
  Thy Light in all I see;
Thou Great God Presence,
  Evermore just Thee;
O Silent Watcher,
  O Love, now speak to me.

O Silent Watcher,
  Lord of Love Supreme!
From Thy Great Heart
  In one Unending Stream,
Thy Great Light flows
  From Thee, Great Sun above;
O Silent Watcher,
  Thou art the Self of Love.

✧ ✧ ✧

THE ARCHANGEL MICHAEL, LORD OF THE SUN

Thou Archangel Michael,
  Lord of the Sun,
I hold my hand high to Thee,
  Thou Holy Great One!
I love Thee, I bless Thee,
  Thou God of Great Might!
Blaze through me, blaze through me,
  Blaze through me Thy Light!
Illumine, perfect me,
  Raise me to Thy Height;
Thou Archangel Michael,
  The Lord of the Sun!

THE "I AM PRESENCE" SPEAKS

I come on the Wings of the Great God Flame
  Into the seeming night.
I wend My Way through infinite space
  Raised high on My Pinions bright.
I bless, I heal, I illumine all things
  With the Radiance of God's own Might.
I blaze, I shine, I call "I AM"!
  The "Diamond Heart of Light!"

I breathe the Perfume of Life Supreme,
  The Glory of God's Delight;
I build, I mold, I guide Life's Stream,
  All beauty I bring to sight.
I dance, I play, I give to all
  Great Jewels from the far, far Height;
I come, I go, I answer each Call
  That looks in Love toward the Light.

✧

THE "PRESENCE"

"I AM" the "Presence,"
the Great Eternal One,
"I AM" the "Presence,"
from the Great, Great Central Sun;
"I AM" the "Presence,"
the Secret Heart of Light,
"I AM" the "Presence,"
the Love Flame blazing bright.

LIGHT

"I AM" *all* Light! *All* Light am I,
In earth and air and sea and sky;
"I AM" the Light of Christ held high!
"I AM" *all* Light! *All* Light am I.

ACKNOWLEDGMENT

Beloved Great God Self,
Come, blaze Thou through me,
Reveal now Thy Presence,
Thy Full Mastery.

Pour through me Thy Love Flame,
My Light Self Supreme!
In Vict'ry transcendent,
Thou "Mighty I AM."

✧

ONENESS

O my Divinity,
Blend Thou with me
That I may blaze forth
Thy Full Victory.
Pour through me Thy Flame,
Thou God Self Supreme,
In Glory Transcendent,
Thou "Mighty I AM."

ACCEPTANCE

"I AM" the deepest Love of God
In Thee, O Holy Blessed One;
"I AM" the Love within Thy Ray,
Thou Golden, Blazing Central Sun!

I feel Thy Breath, Thy Love, Thy Power,
Thy Light enfolds me every hour;
I lift my wings, my Victory won,
And rise now free! Life's journey done.

I fly with Thee throughout all space,
I gaze upon Thee face to face;
I know Thy Love is all of me,
Thou art myself, and "I AM" Thee.

PROTECTION

O Blest "I AM," my way is clear,
Thy Love Supreme stands ever near;
Thy Glorious Presence, "Great I AM,"
Forever is my own God Flame.
Steadfast I stand now facing Thee
And naught can interfere with me;
Thy blazing Love does now enfold
And I Thy very Hand do hold.

✧

The Love that "I AM" greets the Love in you,
And all Love, Light and Perfection come
Instantly through and bless you forever.

✧

THE WAY

"I AM" the "Presence," the Great Eternal One,
"I AM" the Power, the Blazing Central Sun;
"I AM" the Splendor, the Dazzling Rays of Light,
"I AM" the Victory, through Love's All-glorious Might.

RELEASE

I come with Love in the Heart of me,
My Love flows out like a great calm sea;
My Love protects, setting all now free,
For Love "I AM," and "I AM" is Thee.

BLESSING FOR FOOD

"Mighty I AM Presence," accept this food, make it pure and holy. Transmute it into Thy Violet Golden Flame of Divine Love, and see that It purifies and perfects all our bodies with the speed of thought, forever Self-sustained.

✧

MIRACLES

"I AM" these Mighty Miracles
performed through me today!
"I AM" these Mighty Miracles
from within my own God Ray!
"I AM" these Mighty Miracles
come forth in Love to stay!
"I AM" these Mighty Miracles,
the Ascended Masters' Way.

PEACE

I rest serene in Thy Embrace,
I hold Thy Hand, I see Thy Face;
I know each day is under grace,
"I AM" at One with Thee.

"MIGHTY I AM PRESENCE"

Charge, charge, charge,
The Lightning of Thy Love;
Charge, charge, charge!
Raise all in Light above;
Charge, charge, charge!
Let all Thy Presence prove;
Charge, charge, charge!
Thy Love where e'er I move.

Take your full Authority, as a Child of Light! a Son of God! a Being of Living Fire, and rebuke every human creation by the command:

Peace! Peace! Peace! Be still!
"I AM" all Love!
"I AM" all Light!
All doeth now My Will.

✧

(MELODY: "My Bonnie Lies Over the Ocean")

I love Thee, I love Thee, I love Thee!
I love Thee, My Dear Self–that's true;
My Holy, Great Glorious, Real Self,
This old human veil I've stepped through.

Chorus

Thyself–myself
I come now! I come now to You! to You;
Myself–Thyself
Blaze through me! blaze through me,
blaze through.

I love You, I love You, I love You!
My Real Self, My God Self, I do;
My Holy Great Glorious, Light Self,
Blaze through me! blaze through me,
blaze through.

Chorus

Thyself–myself,
I love You, I love You, I do, I do;
Myself! Thyself,
There's now only One! that One–You!

✧✦✧

THE ASCENDED HOSTS' DECREE
FOR
AMERICA

In the Name and by the Power of the Ascended Hosts and the Ascended Master Saint Germain, I voice Their Decree for the Blessing and Protection of our Beloved America. America has been brought into being by the Ascended Hosts, as a Radiating Center to all the world for "the Light of God That Never Fails," in the age which has now begun.

Unto this end, there has been brought into existence a Sacred Document, upon which the Government of the United States of America has been founded. This is the Sacred Constitution of the United States of America. Therefore, it is the Decree of the Ascended Host that every official in our Government shall uphold and defend the Constitution of the United States of America unto the best of his ability, "So help him God."

Thus America shall go forward unto greater Glory than has ever been known on Earth. The Ascended Host, who are All-Powerful throughout the Universe, have decreed, "America shall remain at peace with the world." To those who have sought to draw America into the destruction unto which the rest of the nations of the Earth seem determined to open themselves, the

Ascended Hosts have issued the All-Powerful Command that "America and Her people, those Beloved Children of God who have sought the Light, shall be protected; and that glory which they have earned shall go forth into manifestation."

Thus speaketh the Ascended Hosts unto the children of Earth! Their Decree goes forth unchallenged into manifestation from now on, henceforth and forevermore. In Their Name I have spoken!

Donald Ballard

FINIS

SAINT GERMAIN SERIES

VOLUME 5

Part II

"I AM" DECREES

BY

CHANERA

SAINT GERMAIN PRESS

✧✧✧

THE ASCENDED MASTERS' INSTRUCTION

The "Mighty I AM Presence" is the Law of Life, and Its application by the individual is his Eternal Freedom, Victory, and Mastery over all outer activities of the world.

"I AM" is the Great Creative Word by which form and activity come into outer expression through the individual.

This Ascended Master Instruction is educational rather than religious and teaches the individual the Ascended Master Control of energy and vibration through his own Call to the "Mighty I AM Presence."

An "I AM" Decree is an Acknowledgment of your Divine Authority to command substance and energy to produce Perfection for you, and is Mastery expressed by the Power of Divine Love!

Prayer carries a feeling of lack and is the asking, beseeching consciousness.

The Ascended Masters have said that until mankind makes the Call, the Great Law cannot act, because the Call from the Heart of humanity through the individual is the open door through which the answer must come. The Law of the Ascended Masters'

Octave of Life will not permit Them to intrude into the physical activity of mankind unless invited to do so by the individual.

We ask everyone to do this for the protection of America now, and the Victory of "The Light of God That Never Fails."

They stand ready to give Assistance without limit, but mankind must raise itself by the release of its own Life Energy from within its own Heart. This expands the Light and Love of Life and is obedience to the Great Law of the Universe.

Chanera

✧ ✧ ✧

TO THE READER AND STUDENT

The word "human" in all this Ascended Master Instruction is always used to mean discordant, as distinguished from the Perfection of Divinity. The words "blast" and "annihilate" are never applied to physical bodies.

We want everyone to know that the Ascended Masters never use a destructive force! The "Mighty I AM Presence" never uses a destructive force! We never use a destructive force!

The Action of the Law, when we call the "Mighty I AM Presence" or Ascended Masters to correct any condition that is inharmonious or vicious, is that They project the Sacred Flame of Divine Love into the person, place, condition or thing! This is the highest rate of vibration in the Universe, because It is the most Powerful Use of the Electronic Force of Light.

As It passes through whatever is to be perfected, It simply purifies all by increasing the rate of vibration to the point where no discord can any longer exist, because It draws all Electronic Force into Itself. It being All-Powerful and All Perfection, all rates of vibration less than Itself are annihilated or blasted from existence.

In all this Work, the Student always calls the "Mighty I AM Presence"–which is God in Action–and the Ascended Masters to do whatever is necessary to produce Perfection; for we tell everyone, and all should know that God, the "Mighty I AM Presence," is the *only Doer* of anything that is good–the *only Giver* of anything that is good.

Any other interpretation of this Activity is vicious, willful misrepresentation, and has no power by which to longer exist.

We say to all who read this Book: It does not matter whether you understand this Ascended Master Instruction fully or not. If you will give forth the Decrees in this Book with firm determination and keep your feelings happy and harmonious, with regular use of these Decrees three times a day, you will have all the proof you need to know that this Mighty Instruction of the "I AM" is the Law of Life, and your application of It is your Eternal Freedom.

Through the issuing of these Decrees, everyone within the borders of the United States of America can give Limitless Assistance for Her protection from destructive activities and help call forth the Perfection which She shall express. We ask every human being within Her borders to give this assistance–and give it *now*–for the "Mighty I AM Presence" and the

Ascended Masters say forever to all mankind:

> *"Call unto Me and I will answer you! Decree a thing and it shall be established unto you! Concerning the Works of My Hands, command ye Me! Prove Me now, if I will not open the Windows of Heaven and pour you out a Blessing until there is not room to receive It!"*

These Words have been spoken to mankind for millions of years, because they are the *Eternal Law of the "Mighty I AM Presence"–the Law of Life!*

If the owner of any constructive line of business would call his employees together for five minutes morning and evening, all keeping their feelings happy and harmonious; and give these Decrees for the Protection of America and the Perfection of all business conditions, wonders unbelievable would take place for all concerned!

Chanera

✧ ✧ ✧

DECREES

The Word "I AM" should always be thought, felt, read or spoken with the feeling of an exclamation; for It is the Supreme Presence and Power of Life announcing Itself through the individual, constantly reminding him of his Source, as if saying: "I AM" here!

✧ 1 ✧

ASCENSION

"MIGHTY BLESSED, ADORABLE PRESENCE OF THE I AM"!

Do for all mankind whatever needs to be done now, to make everyone aware of his Blessed "I AM Presence," the Host of Ascended Masters, and of the necessity to make effort to the Ascension.

Great Ascended Masters of Light and Love, Great Cosmic Beings and Great Cosmic Light! charge mankind's consciousness everywhere with Thy Ascended Master Comprehension, Eternal Divine Memory, All-Powerful Concentration, Infinite Patience and Divine Love, until every human being accepts the Fullness of the Ascension and comes through into Victory.

"I AM"! the Resurrection and the Life! "I AM"! the Ascension in the Light now made manifest! Great Host of Ascended Masters, give us the Full Ascended Master Feeling of this now and raise us quickly into Its Eternal Accomplishment; that we may be prepared, return quickly and render assistance without limit everywhere until all are Free!

All that we have decreed and asked for ourselves, we decree and ask for every human being on the Earth and all who come here in the future; that the whole planet may blaze forth the Eternal Victory and Light of the "Mighty I AM Presence" and sing the Eternal Song of Joy, the Ecstasy of Light, and evermore be at peace.

We thank Thee Thou dost always answer our every Call instantly.

✧ 2 ✧

ASCENSION EN MASSE

"MIGHTY I AM PRESENCE," GREAT HOST OF ASCENDED MASTERS, MIGHTY LEGIONS OF LIGHT, GREAT ANGELIC HOST, GREAT COSMIC BEINGS AND GREAT COSMIC LIGHT!

Come forth in Your Mightiest Cosmic Authority and Power of the Unfed Flame! Seize, bind and annihilate all human creation and its cause and effect of everyone under this Radiation. Cut us all free from the magnetic pull of Earth, the things of Earth, and all human creation forever! and enable us to make our Ascension en masse as quickly as possible, that we may be prepared to return and assist those still following on! until all mankind has made the Ascension also.

✧ 3 ✧

ASCENDED MASTER MEMORY

"MIGHTY BELOVED I AM PRESENCE"! Take complete possession of our entire consciousness forever! Make it crystal clear and pure as the Ascended Masters! Charge it with the Ascended Masters' Eternal Divine Memory and All-Knowing, Dazzling, Fathomless, Diamond-shining Mind of God, Thy Blessed Self in Action! Make us comprehend perfectly all the Ascended Masters' Knowledge within these words, and remember them eternally! Illumine everything to us and tell us the Ascended Master Truth concerning all! Show us the *Perfect Thing* to do each moment and make us do it perfectly!

Cut us free from and consume everything that would confuse, bind or limit us or our worlds, from manifesting the Full Perfection of the Ascended Masters and the Victory of our Ascension—*now*! Let every word we speak be a Golden Flame of Divine Love, charged with the "Power of a Thousand Suns" to illumine the consciousness of everyone in the world and all who come here in the future!

O Thou Infinite "Mighty I AM Presence," Great Host of Ascended Masters, Mighty Legions of Light, Great Angelic Host, Great Cosmic Beings and Great Cosmic Light! Come forth in Thy Cosmic Action of the Unfed Flame of Pure Divine Love, and by the Power of the "Three times Three," charge our minds with Ascended Master Clearness, Eternal Divine Memory, Concentration, Patience, and Activity of the All-Knowing Mind of God, the "Mighty I AM Presence" in Dynamic Action, through these our minds and bodies now and forever! Charge forth Full Ascended Master Consciousness, Substance, and Activity in everything we do, and keep it eternally sustained, that the fullness of Thy Perfection may forever express.

This Eternal Truth of the "I AM Presence" *shall be* the only Consciousness within mankind forever. Charge us with the Ascended Masters' Acceptance of this, eternally sustained!

✧ 4 ✧

ASCENDED MASTER QUALITIES

"MIGHTY BLESSED INFINITE I AM PRESENCE," Great Host of Ascended Masters, Mighty Legions of Light, Great Angelic Host, Great Cosmic Beings, and Great Cosmic Light! Come forth in the Limitlessness of Thy Mighty Presence and Cosmic Power into the physical octave of Earth! Charge into the "I AM" Students, the fullness of the Ascended Masters' Love, Light, Wisdom, Power, Infinite Patience, Kindliness, Humility, Reverence, Gratitude, Purity, Spiritual Integrity, and Honor in everything we do–now and forever–eternally sustained by the Ascended Masters' Obedience, Self-control, Management, Marvelous Directing Intelligence, Insight, Foresight, Inspiration, Discrimination, Discretion, Diplomacy, Peace, Poise, and Praise!

Charge us and our worlds with Ascended Master Love, and pour It through us with the "Power of a Thousand Suns" to blaze forth with such irresistible force that all unlike Itself is instantly consumed, Perfection made manifest, and all set Free wherever we move and to whom our thought is directed.

In the Fullest Perfection Earth has ever known, make every "I AM" Student an Ambassador from the Ascended Host of Light! We call to the "I AM

Presence" of each one to take command of his mind and body, produce Perfection and hold Dominion! Let no one betray the Trust that the Ascended Masters give us! Do Thou, our own "I AM Presence," hold our hands, go before us, clear the way, make all things harmonious, prosperous, successful and Perfect. Charge forth in, through, and around us, such Invincible Protection and Almighty Perfection, that we move wholly untouched by anything but Ascended Master Perfection in all our experiences, eternally sustained.

We thank Thee Thou dost always answer our every Call, instantly and infinitely, keeping It eternally sustained and ever-expanding.

✧ 5 ✧

AUTOMOBILE PROTECTION

"MIGHTY I AM PRESENCE," GREAT HOST OF ASCENDED MASTERS, MIGHTY LEGIONS OF LIGHT, GREAT ANGELIC HOST, GREAT COSMIC BEINGS AND GREAT COSMIC LIGHT! Charge every automobile with the Ascended Masters' *Invincible Protection* forever! See that all Students coming to or returning from all Classes and Activities of this Ascended Master Instruction of the "Mighty I AM Presence," are at all times *Invincibly Protected*, supplied without limit, perfectly controlled and directed ONLY by their own "Mighty I AM Presence" and the Ascended Masters! Charge them and all they do under this Radiation forever, with the most Gigantic, Majestic Ascended Master Miracles of Perfection, eternally sustained and ever-expanding Their Joy, Freedom and Light to all!

✧ 6 ✧

AVIATION, TRANSPORTATION, COMMUNICATION, PUBLIC UTILITIES

"MIGHTY I AM PRESENCE," GREAT HOST OF ASCENDED MASTERS, MIGHTY LEGIONS OF LIGHT, GREAT ANGELIC HOST, ANGELS, ANGEL DEVAS, ARCHANGELS, CHERUBIM, SERAPHIM, GREAT ELOHIM OF CREATION, THE LORDS OF THE FLAME FROM VENUS, THE GODS OF THE MOUNTAINS, AND GREAT COSMIC BEINGS!

Come forth in Thy limitless most dynamic Action of the Unfed Flame, the "Three times Three" and the Cosmic Light! Take complete possession and command of every airplane in the United States of America forever! Withdraw and withhold this instant and forever, all energy, money and supply of every kind from every destructive channel, person, place, condition and thing within all activities of aviation, transportation, communication, public utilities, and all channels that supply the necessities of life to mankind! Annihilate all such destructive qualities from existence and blast their cause and effect from the Earth, its atmosphere, and humanity forever! Send a Cherubim and an Angel with the Sword of Blue Flame of Divine Love to abide within and around every airplane in our country–the United States of America! Our Country! The "I AM" Country! The Land of "The Light of God That Never Fails"! to hold the Focus of the Cosmic Light so All-Powerfully within and around every airplane that only Ascended Master Perfection can ever exist within, or touch them and their activities forever! Bring into the outer use of mankind the new planes that are accident proof! All interference with these marvelous channels of transportation, communication and public service shall be annihilated from existence forever! and the Ascended Master Perfection designed for them shall come forth now! in spite of any human being or all human beings on Earth! and Their Perfection and Blessing is eternally sustained!

✧ 7 ✧

ANY CITY

"MIGHTY I AM PRESENCE," GREAT HOST OF ASCENDED MASTERS, MIGHTY LEGIONS OF LIGHT, GREAT ANGELIC HOST, GREAT COSMIC BEINGS! In Thy Cosmic Activity of the Great Quenchless Flame of Divine Love and Thy Eternal Unfed Light, blaze through this city the Mightiest Outpouring of Ascended Master Consciousness, Almighty Perfection and Freedom, that has ever yet come forth on Earth. Blaze forth throughout this city of ____________ Your Mighty Outpouring of Divine Love and Light, so All-controlling that nothing discordant can longer stand before Its Onrush. Take possession of everything in this city. Bring all into Divine Order through Divine Love! Set every individual Free in the Full Conscious Knowledge of his "Mighty I AM Presence" and give him his Ascension as soon as possible.

In the Name of the "Mighty I AM Presence," baptize and drench the city of ______________ with Thy Mighty Cosmic Outpouring of Ascended Master Substance, Divine Love and the Violet Consuming Flame so Almighty and Irresistible that It blazes forth Limitless Mighty Ascended Master Miracles for the Freedom of the world. Make every city in our United

States of America an Alabaster City of "the Light of God that never fails"! We charge this with the Divine Director's Ascended Master Consciousness of Instantaneous Activity and Fulfillment, eternally sustained. We Thank Thee it is done.

✧ 8 ✧

ANY COUNTRY–TO GIVE HELP

"MIGHTY I AM PRESENCE," GREAT HOST OF ASCENDED MASTERS, MIGHTY LEGIONS OF LIGHT, GREAT ANGELIC HOST, GREAT COSMIC BEINGS, GREAT COSMIC LIGHT, SAINT GERMAIN, JESUS, NADA, AND THE GREAT DIVINE DIRECTOR!

Send Your Legions of the Angels of Blue Lightning to sweep everywhere into our Beloved Land (or city of ________________)! Seize, bind, and blast all and its cause and effect that causes discord, destruction and limitation to our people! Replace all such activities by the Ascended Masters' Light Substance, filling all instantly with Divine Justice, Invincible Protection, and Mighty Ascended Master Miracles of Joy and Limitless Perfection, eternally sustained and ever-expanding.

Charge forth through the "I AM" Students and all who sincerely seek the Light Thy Ascended Master Consciousness! Never again permit them to be deceived by any person, place, condition or thing! Never permit them to accept or be influenced by anything less than the Perfection of the "I AM" and the Ascended Masters. Insulate each one in the Magic Electronic Tube of Invincible Protection! Shut out all mistakes of the past! And do Thou, O "Mighty I AM Presence" of each one, stand guard forever! Seize and hold the attention of the entire consciousness of every "I AM" Student, mankind, and all forces within nature upon Thy Eternal Perfection! Cut all free from the magnetic pull of Earth, the things of Earth and all human creation. Make and keep us infinitely sensitive to Thee and Thy Perfection, and absolutely nonrecordant to human creation.

Blaze forth through us such a Powerful Healing Radiance, such an Almighty Purifying Presence, that everywhere we move and the "I AM" Activity is held, those cities become Alabaster Cities of Light and Truth–new Holy Cities on Earth. Focus into them Gigantic Pillars of the combined Love, Light, Substance, Wisdom, and Power of the "Mighty I AM Presence" and the Ascended Masters! Let the Unfed Flame come forth as the Center of each city to hold the Eternal Perfection of the Ascended Masters there forever! Provide those Precipitated Buildings into which the "I AM" Students can come, call forth the Full, Limitless Action and Perfection of the "Presence," and manifest the Victory of Light in everything!

We thank Thee Thou dost always answer our every Call instantly, and it is eternally sustained.

✧ 9 ✧

ANNIHILATE LYING AND DECEIT

"MIGHTY I AM PRESENCE," GREAT HOST OF ASCENDED MASTERS, MIGHTY LEGIONS OF LIGHT, GREAT ANGELIC HOST, GREAT COSMIC BEINGS, AND GREAT COSMIC LIGHT!

Come forth in Your Mightiest Cosmic Action of the Unfed Flame! Annihilate forever the mass entity of lying and deceit, and its cause and effect in all mankind, the Earth and its atmosphere! Annihilate all such qualities in every human being forever, and replace them by the Ascended Masters' Truth, Honesty, Honor, Integrity, and Light Substance, instantly and infinitely manifest, eternally sustained and ever-expanding.

✧ 10 ✧

ARMED FORCES

"MIGHTY I AM PRESENCE," GREAT HOST OF ASCENDED MASTERS, MIGHTY LEGIONS OF LIGHT, GREAT ANGELIC HOST, AND GREAT COSMIC BEINGS DIRECTLY CONCERNED WITH AMERICA! IN THE FULL POWER OF CYCLOPEA, THE ALL-SEEING EYE OF GOD!

Blaze forth Thy Almighty Control of every human being in America! See that everyone in the Armed Forces of America forever remains loyal and gives Invincible Protection to America through "the Light of God that never fails"–in full Conscious Knowledge of the "I AM Presence" and Great Host of Ascended Masters! Bless all in those channels of service with the Ascended Masters' Consciousness, Substance, Mastery, Victory and Perfection of the "Mighty I AM Presence" in the Eternal Cosmic Activity of the Unfed Flame, the "Three times Three" and the Cosmic Light! We thank Thee, Thou dost always answer our every Call!

✧ 11 ✧

ALABASTER CITIES (HOLY CITIES)

"MIGHTY INFINITE I AM PRESENCE," GREAT HOST OF ASCENDED MASTERS, MIGHTY LEGIONS OF LIGHT, GREAT ANGELIC HOST, GREAT COSMIC BEINGS WHO ARE AUTHORITY FOR THE UNITED STATES OF AMERICA!

Come forth in the Full Cosmic Power of the Unfed Flame, the "Three times Three" and the Cosmic Light! Blaze forth the fullness of Thy Limitless Dominion. Release such a Mighty Onrush of Thy Cosmic Light, that It illumines everything unlike Itself and reveals to humanity the Eternal Truth and Law of the "Mighty I AM Presence" everywhere.

Charge forth through our Music the Ascended Masters' Limitless Illumination, Invincible Protection, Inexhaustible Opulence, until there is not room to receive It; Instantaneous Healing, Indestructible Health, Inexhaustible Energy, Everlasting Peace, eternally sustained. Release into use in the outer world the new musical instruments! Let the Pure True Music of the Spheres–vocal and instrumental–pour forth on Earth *now*, through us, and release the Eternal Victory of the Ascension for all. We thank Thee and accept the fullness of this in dynamic action forever, and we know Thou dost always answer our every Call instantly, and keep it eternally sustained!

✧ 12 ✧
APPETITES

"MIGHTY INFINITE I AM PRESENCE," GREAT HOST OF ASCENDED MASTERS, GREAT COSMIC BEINGS, AND GREAT COSMIC LIGHT!

Send Thy Legions of Angels of the Blue Lightning of Divine Love and the Cosmic Activity of the Sword of Blue Flame of Divine Love into the physical octave of Earth! Blast forever from within and around every human being, the Earth and its atmosphere all cravings and desires for alcohol, tobacco, narcotics, and flesh foods! Blast those appetites from humanity for all Eternity! Annihilate their cause and effect! Replace them by the Perfect Food and Satisfaction of the Ascended Masters, and release mankind from the chains of all such vicious activities.

Charge the physical and mental body of every human being, the Earth and its atmosphere with the Substance from the Secret Love Star, and release Its

Satisfying Activity and feeling unto mankind forever!

Blaze forth whatever Activity of the Violet Consuming Flame and the Power of the Blue Lightning of Divine Love is required to annihilate these conditions from the Earth forever! This instant, seize, bind, and take out of the atmosphere of Earth every discarnate entity. Hold them bound and inactive in the Octave of Light, until they surrender everything to their "Mighty I AM Presence" and serve the Light forever! Replace them by Angels of Purity and Perfection, Angels from the Healing Temples and the Almighty Purifying Activity of the Violet Flame! Once again, charge the consciousness of mankind with Ascended Master Intelligence, Self-control, Obedience, and Management of all outer desires and activities! Turn the attention of all to the "Mighty I AM Presence" and blaze forth Thy Full Perfection!

✧ 13 ✧

ANNIHILATION OF ALL GAMBLING

"MIGHTY I AM PRESENCE," GREAT HOST OF ASCENDED MASTERS, GREAT COSMIC BEINGS, GREAT COSMIC LIGHT! MIGHTY ARCHANGEL

MICHAEL, ASTREA AND OROMASIS, AND GREAT LORDS OF THE FLAME FROM VENUS!

Come forth in Your Mightiest Consuming Power of the Blue Lightning and Sword of Blue Flame of Divine Love, and compel all gambling to annihilate itself, and its cause and effect, instantly and eternally from this moment! Cut blessed humanity free from every activity of the psychic plane and blast that viciousness from existence forever! Replace all such activities with the Limitless Light, Love, and Intelligence of the Ascended Masters, and keep It the only acting Consciousness within all forever!

✧ 14 ✧
ATTENTION

"MIGHTY I AM PRESENCE," take possession of all my time, attention, vision, sight, hearing, speech, action, thought, feeling, substance, energy, being and world! Produce the Ascended Masters' Perfection and hold Your Dominion forever in my entire being and world!

✧ 15 ✧

ABNORMAL GROWTH

"MIGHTY I AM PRESENCE," reach Your Hand into this human form; dissolve and consume cause and effect of this unnatural condition or growth, and cause it to disappear from within my world forever!

✧ 16 ✧

ANNIHILATION OF ALL RED AND COMMUNISTIC ACTIVITY

"MIGHTY I AM PRESENCE," GREAT HOST OF ASCENDED MASTERS, MIGHTY LEGIONS OF LIGHT, GREAT ANGELIC HOST, GREAT COSMIC BEINGS, AND GREAT COSMIC LIGHT!

Blaze forth whatever Power of the Blue Lightning and Sword of the Blue Flame of Divine Love is required to Blast from existence forever all red and communistic teaching, all destructive activity and its cause and effect from humanity, the Earth, and its atmosphere this very instant! Withdraw and withhold all energy, money, power, supply, and influence of every kind from those channels and make them annihilate themselves from existence on this Earth forever! Replace them by the Visible, Tangible, Living, Breathing Presence and Perfection of the Ascended Masters, eternally sustained, for the Freedom and Blessing of all mankind and the Earth forever!

We thank Thee the Victory of Light of all Ages is now come to pass! Great Cosmic Light! Take Eternal Possession of the Earth and all that is herein! Produce Perfection and hold Your Dominion here forever!

✧ 17 ✧

BLESSING SAINT GERMAIN AND ALL ASCENDED MASTERS

"MIGHTY I AM PRESENCE" OF THE GREAT CENTRAL SUN! We call forth the Mightiest Cosmic Light and Power from Thy Heart to bless our Beloved Ascended Masters: Saint Germain, Jesus, Nada, the Great Divine Director, Sanat Kumara, and all Ascended Masters, and Great Beings of Light who have guarded and assisted the children of Earth through the centuries!

We offer to Them all the Eternal Love and Gratitude from mankind and bless Them forever!

✧ 18 ✧

BLESSING OF THE UNITED STATES OF AMERICA

"MIGHTY INFINITE I AM PRESENCE," THOU MIGHTY GUARDIAN PRESENCE FOR AMERICA!

Come forth in Thy Cosmic Action of the Unfed Flame of Divine Love and the Eternal Quenchless Light! Blaze forth everywhere in and through our Beloved Americas, Thy Light as of a Thousand Suns, charged with Ascended Master Consciousness and Fulfillment of the Divine Plan for their Freedom and Perfection.

We say to the consciousness of everyone in the Americas: "Awake! awake! awake! to the Truth of this 'Mighty I AM Presence' and the Full Perfection meant for the Americas." Great Ones! release throughout them that Activity of Thy Light which takes possession everywhere of the Americas, the governments and the people. Control their resources, direct their activities, fill them with Thy lavish abundance of all good things, and release that Ascended Master Consciousness which compels Divine Justice to come forth for everyone within their borders. Surround them with Thy Invincible Protection! Blaze forth Thy Mighty Activity of the Light and Love of the Ascended Masters and the Angelic Host, that once and forever brings all into Divine Order through Divine Love! Charge forth Thy Full Perfection everywhere forever!

In the Name of the "Mighty I AM Presence," we decree that the Americas shall be manifest as Nations of Ascended Masters, to lead the rest of the Earth into their Eternal Glory and the Victory of the Ascension.

America, we love you! America, we love you! America, we love you! And our Love and call to the "Mighty I AM Presence" is great enough to bring forth Your Perfection *now*, and keep It forever sustained. We charge you, our Beloved America, with the Ascended Masters' Eternal Victory of "The Light of God That Never Fails," and the Mighty Mastery of the "I AM Presence" expanding Its Perfection everywhere within Your borders. So long as the Stars remain and the Heavens send down dew, so long shall our Beloved, Beloved America carry the "Grail of Light" high, and feed the rest of the Earth with the Ascended Masters' Outpouring of Freedom and Perfection of the "Mighty I AM Presence."

America! we enfold you in our Mantle of Light and Love! Within It is All Power. We hold you sealed within our Hearts, and Your Mighty Victory shall manifest every hour, to the Glory of the "I AM" and the Ascended Ones forever!

✧ 19 ✧

BLESSING FOR OUR FLAG

"MIGHTY I AM PRESENCE," GREAT HOST OF ASCENDED MASTERS, MIGHTY LEGIONS OF LIGHT, GREAT ANGELIC HOST, AND MIGHTY COSMIC BEINGS WHO GUARD OUR BELOVED UNITED STATES OF AMERICA!

Charge forth into the feeling of everyone within our borders the Ascended Masters' Consciousness, Love, and Loyalty to the United States of America! Our Country! The "I AM" Country! God's Country! The Land of "the Light of God that never fails!" Drench them with the Ascended Masters' Light Substance and Respect for our Flag! Compel everything unlike that to annihilate itself from within our borders this moment and forever! Release through the Hearts and minds of everyone within our borders whatever Light and Love is necessary to do this now, and keep it forever self-sustained! We thank Thee it is done!

✧ 20 ✧

BLESSING THE AMERICAS

"MIGHTY BLESSED BELOVED I AM PRESENCE," GREAT HOST OF ASCENDED MASTERS, MIGHTY LEGIONS OF LIGHT, AND GREAT ANGELIC HOST, GREAT COSMIC BEINGS, GREAT COSMIC LIGHT, AND GREAT PRESENCE WHO GUARD OUR BELOVED AMERICA!

Come forth in Thy full Power of the Unfed Flame, the "Three times Three" and the Cosmic Light! Take possession of the Americas, their governments and their people. Control their resources, direct their activities, give them Invincible Protection, Limitless Supply, Infinite Cosmic Light, Almighty Ascended Master Consciousness, Infallible Directing Intelligence in all they do, and the Fullness of Your Power of Divine Love acting everywhere in the physical life of all the Americas.

Produce Your Perfection! Hold Your Dominion! Flood them with Your Light Substance, and let the Americas stand as Nations of Ascended Masters, releasing their Light to the rest of the Earth until all mankind is Free.

To You, our Beloved United States of America–and the Americas–we say: America, we love you!

America, we love you! America, we love you with a Love that is Infinite, Eternal, and Almighty! Our Love shall guard you with Invincible Power forever, forever, and forever, against everything that is less than the Ascended Masters' Perfection! "The Light of God That Never Fails" shall rule forever within the Americas, and so long as the Stars remain and the Heavens send down dew, so long shall the Americas remain the "Land of Light and Love."

I have spoken in the Name of the "Mighty Infinite I AM Presence." I have commanded by the Power of the Unfed Flame, the "Three times Three" and the Cosmic Light, and so shall it be established to the people of the Americas forever. We thank Thee!

✧ 21 ✧

BLESSING COMING CLASSES AND AUDITORIUMS

"MIGHTY I AM PRESENCE," GREAT HOST OF ASCENDED MASTERS, MIGHTY LEGIONS OF LIGHT, GREAT ANGELIC HOST, GREAT COSMIC BEINGS, GREAT COSMIC LIGHT, AND THE SEVEN MIGHTY ELOHIM OF CREATION!

Come forth in Your Full Cosmic Authority! By

the Power of the Unfed Flame, the "Three times Three," and the Great Cosmic Light, bless the (coming) ________________ "I AM" Class and the ________________ Auditorium with such an Outpouring of Cosmic Light, Love, and Blessings to the Messengers, the Students, the people of ________________ (city), America, and the world, as has never been experienced on Earth! Flood forth such Miracles of Instantaneous Healing, Protection, Illumination, Limitless Financial Abundance, and every good thing! Freedom, Victory, and Perfection! that the most Transcendent Accomplishment ever known on this planet will take place! Reach out Your Great Loving Arms! Draw all here who can be benefited through this Focus of Light! Keep away all others! See that the Auditorium is filled to overflowing with earnest seekers of the Light, so that the greatest good may be accomplished in the shortest time possible. Prepare all and make all worthy to partake of this Mighty Outpouring of Divine Love. We thank Thee Thou dost always answer our every Call. *(Visualize the Auditorium as a Palace of Light, made of myriad of diamonds blazing out a Dazzling Golden-white Radiance for many miles in every direction! See multitudes of people coming from every quarter to receive enormous Blessings and to gain their Eternal Freedom.)*

✧ 22 ✧

BLESSING TO THE INHABITANTS OF THE ELEMENTS

"MIGHTY I AM PRESENCE," GREAT HOST OF ASCENDED MASTERS, MIGHTY LEGIONS OF LIGHT, GREAT ANGELIC HOST, AND GREAT COSMIC BEINGS!

Pour forth through us Thy Limitless Blessings of Love, Light, Joy, Gratitude, and Eternal Perfection to all the inhabitants of the Elements and those Great Ascended Beings who govern Their Activities for their constant Service and Blessing to the mankind of Earth forever!

✧ 23 ✧

BLESSING BUSINESS

"MIGHTY I AM PRESENCE"! CHARGE! CHARGE! CHARGE! CHARGE us and the business world with the Pure Electronic Substance from the Ascended Masters' Octave of Life, the Secret Love Star and the Golden City, to bring Balance, Purity, and Perfection everywhere. Let Thy Divine Justice come forth! Take possession of *all* business activities, and compel them to give Divine Justice to every human being on the Earth; that Thy Blazing Glory, Freedom, Eternal Joy, Protection and the Victory of the Ascension may come forth throughout the Earth for the freedom and happiness of all. We thank Thee Thou dost always answer our Call instantly, and It is eternally sustained and ever-expanding.

✧ 24 ✧

BUSINESS ACTIVITY

"MIGHTY INFINITE I AM PRESENCE," GREAT HOST OF ASCENDED MASTERS! Charge forth into the commercial world everywhere Your Ascended Master Consciousness of Purity, Balance, Divine Justice, Perfect Success and Activity *for every constructive thing in all business channels right now,* by the Power of Thy Love that is Irresistible! Withdraw all energy from all destructive activities in all commercial channels! Charge that energy with the Ascended Masters' Consciousness, Substance, Perfection, Invincible Protection, Limitless Supply, and Almighty Power of "The Light of God That Never Fails"! Hold that energy within this Ascended Master Activity of the "I AM" to produce Perfection everywhere for the Freedom and Illumination of all humanity! Charge forth the feeling into all business channels of the Ascended Masters' Consciousness and desire to give everybody Divine Justice and make mankind forever incapable of doing anything else! We charge this Decree forth with the Power of a Thousand Suns, to take possession of the feeling of humanity everywhere, to produce Perfection and hold its Dominion forever. We thank Thee Thou dost always answer our every Call instantly!

✧ 25 ✧

CHARGING OUR RADIO BROADCASTS

"MIGHTY I AM PRESENCE," GREAT HOST OF ASCENDED MASTERS, MIGHTY LEGIONS OF LIGHT, GREAT ANGELIC HOST, AND GREAT COSMIC BEINGS!

Come forth in Your Full Cosmic Authority and Power of the Unfed Flame, the "Three times Three" and the Cosmic Light!

Charge all our radio broadcasts with the Mightiest Power of the Ascended Masters' Light, Love, and Substance Earth has ever experienced! Charge every word that goes over the air with Saint Germain, Jesus, Nada, and the Divine Director's Ascended Master Consciousness, Instantaneous Activity and Fulfillment, eternally sustained! Charge forth through these broadcasts the Fullness of the Flame of Light and Love from all the Hosts of Light, in the most Irresistible Onrush of "The Light of God That Never Fails," in the Full Cosmic Power of the Blue Ray and Blue Lightning of Divine Love! See that the Words, "I AM" register in Letters of Eternal Living Fire in the mental and feeling world of every human being on Earth! Charge all mankind with the Ascended Masters' Comprehension of all the "I AM" means to humanity! Awaken everyone throughout the world to this Mighty Light and Freedom of the "Mighty I AM Presence," and hold them within Its Heart forever! Cover our United States of America with the Presence of the "Unfed Flame," and see that It consumes all that is not the Ascended Masters' Perfection for Her forever! We thank Thee it is done instantly!

✧ 26 ✧

CHARGING ENERGY IN GAS BELTS

"MIGHTY I AM PRESENCE," GREAT HOST OF ASCENDED MASTERS, MIGHTY LEGIONS OF LIGHT, GREAT ANGELIC HOST, GREAT COSMIC BEINGS, MIGHTY GODS OF THE MOUNTAINS, TABOR, MERU, HIMALAYA, AND THE ONE IN CHARGE OF THE SWISS ALPS, MIGHTY GOD OF NATURE, GREAT GOD OF GOLD!

Come forth in Your Full Cosmic Authority! by the Power of the Unfed Flame, the "Three times Three," and the Great Cosmic Light, seize control of all the energy in the Gas Belts throughout the Earth and turn it all into pure metallic gold! Let its Radiation come through to purify the substance of Earth, its atmosphere, all nature, and the bodies of mankind! Let all be filled now with that Pure Energy and bring Your Perfect Balance into all outer activity for mankind and the Earth, eternally sustained and ever-expanding.

✧ 27 ✧

COMPREHENSION AND CONCENTRATION

"MIGHTY I AM PRESENCE"! Charge me with the Ascended Masters' Crystal Clear Comprehension, Eternal Divine Memory, Infinite Patience, All-powerful Concentration and the All-loving Heart of God in my every thought, feeling, and spoken word forever.

✧ 28 ✧

CLEANLINESS

"MIGHTY I AM PRESENCE," GREAT HOST OF ASCENDED MASTERS, MIGHTY LEGIONS OF LIGHT, GREAT ANGELIC HOST, GREAT COSMIC BEINGS, AND GREAT COSMIC LIGHT!

Release continuously into and through my being and world and all within it Your Purifying, Illumining Power of the Cosmic Light! Charge everything in my being and world with absolute spotlessness and immaculate cleanliness! Keep everything in Perfect

Ascended Master Condition, eternally sustained! We thank Thee Thou dost always answer our every Call instantly, infinitely and eternally.

✧ 29 ✧

COLORS

"MIGHTY I AM PRESENCE," GREAT HOST OF ASCENDED MASTERS, MIGHTY ELOHIM OF CREATION!

Annihilate the use of all colors of black, destructive shades of red, and dull, impure colors everywhere within and around humanity, the Earth and its atmosphere instantly! Replace these destructive rates of vibration forever by the Pure, True, Perfect Colors of the Ascended Masters' Octave of Life, and reveal to mankind the Mighty Perfection which is the Divine Beauty and Plan of Life!

✧ 30 ✧

CHILDREN

O THOU "INFINITE MIGHTY I AM PRESENCE," GREAT HOST OF ASCENDED MASTERS, MIGHTY LEGIONS OF LIGHT, MIGHTY ANGELIC HOST, GREAT COSMIC BEINGS, AND GREAT COSMIC LIGHT!

We make the Call unto Thee as never before to release Thy Blue Lightning of Divine Love and Thy Sword of Blue Flame of Divine Love! Cut every child and young person on this planet forever free from every force, condition, and thing that would be unjust or bind them into destructive activities in any way!

In the Name of the "Mighty I AM Presence, we claim every child and young person on the face of the Earth into the Service of the Light of the "Mighty I AM Presence" and Ascended Host! We call forth whatever Activity of the Great Cosmic Law is required to seize, bind, and annihilate all that interferes with their full expression of the Ascended Masters' Perfection! We speak directly to the Electronic Body of every young person on Earth to blaze forth the Ascended Masters' Activity of the Sword of Blue Flame of Divine Love, and cut them free from everything that would draw them from the Pathway of Light! Annihilate all injustice and every discordant thing by which they are now surrounded. Lift them completely into the Octave of Light of the Ascended Masters and blast all teaching from the Earth that is not the Eternal Truth of the "Mighty I AM Presence" and Great Host of Ascended Masters! Charge forth Thy Mighty Illumination into every brain and body! Charge them with Ascended Master Obedience, Self-control, Management, Marvelous Directing Intelligence and Strength that refuses acceptance to everything but Ascended Master Perfection. Clothe them in Thy Mighty Glory which keeps them forever invisible, invincible, and invulnerable to everything that does not serve the Light! Let these precious ones go forth completely released to render that service to the Earth which brings forth the Golden Age, and bless them with the Fullness of the Ascended Masters' Divine Love, Limitless Light, Strength, Perfection, and the Victory of their Ascension!

In the Name of the "Mighty I AM Presence," I have spoken! And so shall it be established unto them!

✧ 31 ✧

DAILY CALL

"MIGHTY I AM PRESENCE," AND GREAT HOST OF ASCENDED MASTERS! Stand guard over me this day and forever! See that I am never surprised nor off guard! that I never fail nor make a mistake in a single thing! that no person, place, condition or thing deceives me! that there is nothing hidden that is not revealed to me! Illumine everything to me, show me the Perfect thing to do, and make me do it perfectly; and see that I never miss or disobey a prompting from Thee! Make and keep me infinitely sensitive to Thee and Thy Perfection, and absolutely non-recordant to human creation! Cut me free from the magnetic pull of Earth, the things of Earth and all human creation! See that I never doubt, fear, question, nor am uncertain concerning Thy Instantaneous Fulfillment of my every Call to Thee, My "Beloved I AM"!

✧ 32 ✧

DECREE–FOR ANY CITY AND AMERICA

"MIGHTY I AM PRESENCE," GREAT HOST OF ASCENDED MASTERS, MIGHTY LEGIONS OF LIGHT, GREAT ANGELIC HOST, GREAT COSMIC BEINGS, AND GREAT COSMIC LIGHT!

In Thy Cosmic Activity of the Unfed Flame in Its most dynamic Action, blaze forth Thy Mighty Light as of a Thousand Suns, to illumine everyone here in ________ , America, and the Earth, with such a Mighty Onrush of Ascended Master Perfection that nothing can stand before the Mighty Power of Its Presence and Activity.

Seize possession of the United States of America, the government and Her people! Control Her resources! Release Thy Light and Activity of the "Mighty I AM Presence" everywhere within Her borders and place in office *only* those who serve the Light–"The Light of God That Never Fails"! Hold Thy Active Possession and Dominion within America and Her people forever! Lead Her unto the Height, and make Her become the Ascended Master Nation of the Earth! Make Her people all Ascended Masters–that Nation which Saint Germain has for so many centuries desired to bring forth!

America, we love you! America, we bless you! America, you are the "Cup of Light," the Mighty Holy Grail of the Ascended Masters' Light and Love! Flood the Earth with Your Dazzling Radiance and set all mankind Free!

We thank Thee, Thou Unfed Flame, for the Instantaneous Manifestation and Fulfillment of this which we have decreed! We thank Thee it is done and forever sustained!

✧ 33 ✧

DEBT

"MIGHTY I AM PRESENCE," GREAT HOST OF ASCENDED MASTERS, MIGHTY LEGIONS OF LIGHT, GREAT ANGELIC HOST, AND GREAT COSMIC BEINGS!

Come forth in Your Full Cosmic Authority and Power of the Unfed Flame, the "Three times Three" and the Cosmic Light! Blaze the Blue Lightning and Sword of Blue Flame of Divine Love into the mass entity of debt throughout the world! Annihilate all debts of humanity, individual, national and international, and their cause and effect, from the consciousness of every individual on Earth forever! Release Thy

Limitless Supply of every good thing into everyone's use forever as Your Glad-free Gift of Love! and see all is used in the Service of the Light forever! Bring Perfect Balance everywhere through Divine Love, and keep it forever sustained! Compel every human being on Earth to give and receive Divine Justice to and from all! We thank Thee Thou dost always answer our every Call instantly forever!

✧ 34 ✧

DIVINE LOVE

"MIGHTY I AM PRESENCE," GREAT HOST OF ASCENDED MASTERS, MIGHTY LEGIONS OF LIGHT, GREAT COSMIC BEINGS, GREAT COSMIC LIGHT, GREAT ANGELIC HOST, ANGELS, ANGEL DEVAS AND ARCHANGELS, CHERUBIM, SERAPHIM, AND THE GREAT LORDS OF THE FLAME FROM VENUS!

Come forth in the Mightiest Power of Divine Love the Earth has ever known! Establish Thy Unfed Flame here, in every Sanctuary, in every home on this Earth, and keep It forever sustained! Teach and show every human being the Fullness of Its Mighty Power,

Perfection, and Dominion! Charge forth through every human Heart the full Flame of Divine Love and Joy from each one's own "Mighty I AM Presence"! So expand Its Light and Cosmic Activity through the individual that all will feel and know the Mighty Victory of Its Presence forever! We thank Thee this is done *now*, forever sustained and ever-expanding!

✧ 35 ✧

ETERNAL VICTORY FOR ALL

"MIGHTY I AM PRESENCE," GREAT HOST OF ASCENDED MASTERS, AND ALL GREAT BEINGS OF LIGHT THROUGHOUT INFINITY!

Come forth into the physical octave of Earth and lead the Children of Light through quickly into Eternal Victory! Blaze forth Thy Almighty Power! Charge them with the Ascended Masters' Limitless, Inexhaustible Energy, the full supply of every good thing, Invincible Protection, Indestructible Health, Absolute Courage, and give them the Scepter of Eternal Power to blaze the Light everywhere with Instantaneous Victory and Fulfillment of every Conscious Command of the "I AM." Take them through into their Ascension! that they may render the greatest assistance possible to humanity and the Earth *now*, when it is needed most. We thank Thee it is done and eternally sustained!

Blessed Adorable Sanat Kumara! before Thou and Thy Blessed Ones return to Venus, we ask Thee to come forth in the Tangible Body and walk and talk face to face with the "I AM" Students throughout the world! that they may *feel* Thy Mighty Love, and pour back to Thee that which Thou hast poured to humanity through the centuries!

Blaze forth through each one of the "I AM" Students Thy Flame of Divine Love and expand It to fill the world of each one with the Blazing Perfection which Thou art! In Everlasting Love and Gratitude we Bless Thee for Thy Love to the children of Earth. May each one become a Lord of the Flame as Thou art! In Everlasting Love we bless Thee.

✧ 36 ✧

ETERNAL YOUTH AND BEAUTY

"MIGHTY I AM PRESENCE," GREAT HOST OF ASCENDED MASTERS, MIGHTY LEGIONS OF LIGHT, GREAT ANGELIC HOST, GREAT COSMIC BEINGS AND GREAT COSMIC LIGHT!

Charge me and all whom I contact with Your Marvelous Ascended Master Eternal Youth, Beauty, Inexhaustible Strength, Energy, Indestructible Health, Limitless Joy, Humor and Perfection, expanding Thy Glory to all forever!

✧ **37** ✧

ETERNAL PROTECTION FOR AMERICA

"MIGHTY I AM PRESENCE," GREAT HOST OF ASCENDED MASTERS, MIGHTY LEGIONS OF LIGHT, GREAT ANGELIC HOST, AND GREAT COSMIC BEINGS!

Come forth now in Your Mightiest Authority and Power of the Unfed Flame, the "Three times Three" and the Cosmic Light; take possession forever of the Constitution, the Declaration of Independence, the Supreme Court of the United States of America and all their activities! Produce Your Ascended Master Perfection! Hold Your Dominion, and charge forth Your Invincible, most Dynamic Protection, All-Powerfully in all concerning them, and keep It eternally sustained! Compel every person, place, condition and thing within the government of the United States of America to guarantee and give Divine Justice to every human being on Earth forever; and hold all within the Power of the Blue Ray and Blue Lightning of Divine Love until they do! Blast all epidemics, plagues, vermin, blight and their cause and effect from America, Her people and nature; and stop all rude destructive activities within our borders forever!

✧ 38 ✧

FEAR, DOUBT, AND GRIEF ENTITIES

"MIGHTY I AM PRESENCE," GREAT HOST OF ASCENDED MASTERS, MIGHTY LEGIONS OF LIGHT, GREAT ANGELIC HOST, GREAT COSMIC BEINGS, AND GREAT COSMIC LIGHT!

Blast! blast! blast! forever all entities and their cause and effect–individual and en masse–of doubt, fear, grief, hate, jealousy, criticism, anger, irritation, resentment, and discord of every kind within the thought and feeling of all mankind forever! Annihilate all such qualities from the memory of every human being on Earth forever! and replace them by the Ascended Masters' Victory and Mastery of Light and

Love, eternally sustained! Take into oblivion forever all that does not serve the Light and save blessed, beloved humanity in spite of itself and its creation! By the Power of the Unfed Flame of Divine Love and the Cosmic Light, annihilate every rate of vibration from the bodies of humanity that manifests as a destructive quality, and fill its place with the Pure Electronic Substance of Light from the Ascended Masters' Octave of Life, and keep It forever sustained!

✧ 39 ✧

FINANCIAL HELP–DIRECT

"MIGHTY I AM PRESENCE" AND GREAT HOSTS OF ASCENDED MASTERS! Release into my hands and use today $________ as a Glad-free gift of Love! Give me ten times more than I need, and see that I use it all in the Service of the Light forever! Remove all obstruction and its cause and effect in my feeling that might delay or prevent this instantaneous release into my use! I thank Thee Thou dost always answer my every Call!

✧ 40 ✧

FINANCIAL–DAILY USE

"MIGHTY I AM PRESENCE" AND GREAT HOST OF ASCENDED MASTERS! Open Your own Channel of Limitless Money to me *this very hour!* Keep my being and world always flooded with ten times more money and supply than I need, as Your Glad-free Gift of Love, and see that I always use it in the Service of the Light. I thank Thee Thou dost always fulfill my every Call instantly.

✧ 41 ✧

GENERAL

"MIGHTY I AM PRESENCE"! Come forth here and take possession! Give me *Invincible Protection*! Hold control of my feelings! Charge forth Your Dominion! and keep It eternally sustained!

✧ 42 ✧

HEART OF LOVE

"MIGHTY I AM PRESENCE"! Take possession of my intellectual consciousness and my feeling. Charge me with the Ascended Masters' All-knowing Mind of God and Its Mighty Directing Intelligence. Charge me with Your All-controlling Heart of Love, Ascended Master Obedience, and Self-control eternally sustained! We thank Thee Thou dost always answer our every Call!

✧ 43 ✧

HARMONY IN FAMILIES

"MIGHTY I AM PRESENCE," GREAT HOST OF ASCENDED MASTERS, MIGHTY LEGIONS OF LIGHT, GREAT ANGELIC HOST, GREAT COSMIC BEINGS AND GREAT COSMIC LIGHT! COME FORTH IN YOUR MIGHTIEST POWER OF THE VIOLET CONSUMING FLAME!

Blast forever all and its cause and effect that causes discord or unhappiness of any kind between parents and children, husbands and wives, and in all family relationships! Replace all such activity by *the Ascended Masters' Feeling of Loving Cooperation and Complete Freedom* by that Divine Love which transcends every human concept, and with the Power of a Thousand Suns, release the Eternal Victory and Freedom from within Its Heart, Self-sustained and ever-expanding.

✧ 44 ✧

HEALING ANGELS

"MIGHTY I AM PRESENCE," MIGHTY HOST OF ASCENDED MASTERS AND GREAT HOST OF HEALING ANGELS!

Direct Your Mighty Flames of Light and Love in Their Cosmic Action and Healing Power throughout the mental, emotional, and physical bodies of every human being in the Americas and throughout the world! Annihilate the cause and effect of all epidemics and disease! Blast the fear and sinister hypnotic suggestion that causes them! Charge the minds, bodies, and feelings of the people with the Ascended Masters' Purity, Substance, and Consciousness, the Substance from the Secret Love Star and the Golden City! Charge this forth so powerfully that It consumes everything unlike Itself, and blessed, beloved humanity looks once again unto the Light of Freedom, reaches up, takes its Scepter of Dominion, and comes forth the "Victorious Presence of the Mighty I AM," Lord of Life, Eternally Free!

Charge forth through us the Fullness of the Ascended Masters' Light, Love and Instantaneous Healing Power into all such conditions! Produce Perfection and hold Your Dominion forever. We thank Thee Thou dost always answer our every Call instantly, and keep it eternally sustained and ever-expanding.

✧ 45 ✧

HEALTH AND LAW OF FORGIVENESS

"MIGHTY I AM PRESENCE," GREAT HOST OF ASCENDED MASTERS, MIGHTY LEGIONS OF LIGHT, GREAT ANGELIC HOST, MIGHTY COSMIC BEINGS, AND THE GREAT BEINGS FROM THE HEALING TEMPLE OF LIGHT!

Come forth in *Your Mightiest Combined Healing Power*! We call on the *Law of Forgiveness* for ourselves and all mankind, and we forgive all mistakes of all mankind forever! Blaze forth through every human body on Earth the most Instantaneous Activity and Purifying Power of the Violet Consuming Flame! Annihilate the cause and effect of all disease from humanity forever! Produce Ascended Master Healings and Perfection for all and hold Your Dominion forever! We thank Thee Thou dost always answer our every Call, and it is eternally sustained and ever-expanding.

✧ 46 ✧

HOURLY CALL

"MIGHTY I AM PRESENCE," GREAT HOST OF ASCENDED MASTERS, MIGHTY LEGIONS OF LIGHT, GREAT ANGELIC HOST, GREAT COSMIC BEINGS AND GREAT COSMIC LIGHT!

Come forth everywhere in the Earth and its atmosphere and do Your Perfect Work this very hour! We thank Thee, Thou dost always answer our every Call instantly, and it is eternally sustained and ever-expanding.

✧ 47 ✧

INTERFERENCE WITH THE LIGHT–A

"MIGHTY I AM PRESENCE," GREAT HOST OF ASCENDED MASTERS, MIGHTY LEGIONS OF LIGHT, GREAT ANGELIC HOST, GREAT COSMIC BEINGS AND GREAT COSMIC LIGHT!

Come forth in Your Mightiest Cosmic Power of the Blue Ray, the Blue Lightning and the Sword of Blue Flame of Divine Love! Compel all that consciously opposes or intentionally works against, plagiarizes, deletes, distorts, or misrepresents this Work in any way, to annihilate itself and blast its own cause and effect from existence forever! Cut all instantly and forever free who are under the hypnotic dominating control of those opposed to this Work! Answer every attempted interference with this Expansion of the Light of the "Mighty I AM Presence" with ten thousand times more Light! Set ten thousand times more people Free in the Eternal Victory of their Ascension, by the Full Power of the Blue Ray and the Sword of Blue Flame of Divine Love! Move forward in Your Limitless Cosmic Power and Authority! Set mankind Free right *now* in spite of any human being or all human beings on Earth! All mankind shall serve the Light of the "Mighty

I AM Presence" and be Free in the Full Power of the Ascended Masters forever sustained! We thank Thee it is done!

✧ 48 ✧

INTERFERENCE WITH THE LIGHT–B

"MIGHTY I AM PRESENCE," GREAT HOST OF ASCENDED MASTERS, MIGHTY LEGIONS OF LIGHT, GREAT ANGELIC HOST, GREAT COSMIC BEINGS AND GREAT COSMIC LIGHT!

Answer every attempted interference with this Expansion of the Light of the "Mighty I AM Presence" with ten thousand times more Light! Set ten thousand times more people Free in the Eternal Victory of their Ascension, by the Full Power of the Blue Ray and the Sword of Blue Flame of Divine Love! Move forward in Your Limitless Cosmic Power and Authority! Set mankind Free right now in spite of any human being or all human beings on Earth! All mankind shall serve the Light of the "Mighty I AM Presence" and be Free in the Full Power of the Ascended Masters forever. We thank Thee it is done, Self-sustained and ever-expanding!

✧ 49 ✧

INTERFERENCE WITH MAKING ASCENSION

"MIGHTY I AM PRESENCE," GREAT HOST OF ASCENDED MASTERS, MIGHTY LEGIONS OF LIGHT, GREAT ANGELIC HOST, GREAT COSMIC BEINGS, AND GREAT COSMIC LIGHT!

By the Mighty Cosmic Activity of the Quenchless Flame of Divine Love in Its most Dynamic Action, seize, bind, and remove from the Earth forever every activity, condition, force, and thing that tries to interfere with the Ascension of all mankind! Charge forth such a Mighty Onrush of Thy Cosmic Light, that mankind does make its Ascension quickly into the "I AM Presence" for Its Eternal Freedom! We, the Students of the "I AM," claim every young person in America into the Service of the Light for their own Eternal Freedom and Happiness. We expand this Command to include all humanity! We thank Thee Thou dost *always* answer our every Call.

✧ 50 ✧

INSANITY, SEX, HATE, JEALOUSY, ANGER, IRRITATION, CRITICISM, JUDGMENT, CONDEMNATION

THOU "INFINITE MIGHTY I AM PRESENCE," GREAT HOST OF ASCENDED MASTERS, GREAT COSMIC MESSENGERS, GREAT COSMIC LIGHT, AND THE ANGELS OF BLUE LIGHTNING OF DIVINE LOVE!

Come forth in Your Combined Activity with the Mightiest Power Earth has ever known! Blast from human consciousness, the Earth and its atmosphere, all wrong sex activity, and annihilate its cause and effect forever. Replace it by the Eternal Purity of the Ascended Masters, and release mankind into the Divine Way of Life.

Come forth and annihilate all conditions, and their cause and effect, that produce insanity! Seize, bind, and remove every discarnate entity in and around every human body, the Earth and its atmosphere! Take them to the Octave of Light this very moment, and hold them bound and inactive until they serve the Light. Come forth and remove from all human beings all desires that are less than the Perfection of the "I AM Presence," and fill all with the Satisfaction and Ecstasy of the Ascended Masters! Set all individuals free with the Limitless Strength of the Ascended Masters to come quickly into the Light of the "Mighty I AM Presence," gain their Victory, make the Ascension and be Free!

Come forth in Thy Mighty Cosmic Action, O Great Beings from out the Great Silence! and by the use of Thy Sword of Blue Flame of Divine Love in Its Cosmic Activity, annihilate the mass accumulation of hate, anger, jealousy, resentment, irritation of every kind, criticism, condemnation, and judgment! Purify all that Energy and Substance in the atmosphere of Earth! Annihilate the cause and effect of those qualities within every human being. Replace them by the Fullness of the Divine Love, Light, Wisdom, Power, Self-control, and Obedience of the Ascended Masters, and hold Possession and Dominion within the emotional bodies of mankind forever! Charge them with Ascended Master Light Substance and "The Light of God that never fails," and make that Light so bright that It consumes all unlike Itself! Charge the atmosphere of Earth with the Lightning of Thy Divine Love, and release Thy Purity everywhere!

Seize control of the attention of the people! Focus it upon their own Electronic Bodies of the "Mighty I AM Presence" and the Ascended Masters! Draw them up by the Power of Divine Love into the Mighty Purity and Perfection of their Eternal Victory of the Ascension!

In the Name of the "Mighty I AM Presence," *this Fiat goes forth, and It shall be fulfilled* for the Freedom, Happiness, Victory of all, the Glory of the "I AM," and the Ascended Ones forever.

✧ 51 ✧
JUSTICE

O THOU "MIGHTY INFINITE I AM PRESENCE," THOU SUPREME JUSTICE OF THE UNIVERSE! BY THE POWER OF THE UNFED FLAME, THE "THREE TIMES THREE," AND THE COSMIC LIGHT, let Thy Judgment descend into the physical octave of Earth, and compel Divine Justice to be released this instant into every business activity and be forever sustained! Let Divine Judgment descend on all destructive forces this very moment and annihilate them, their cause and effect from the Earth and mankind forever!

Thou who art Supreme Justice, the Supreme Owner of all that is; the Supreme Giver of all that is; the Supreme Perfection of all that is, and the Supreme Doer of all that is good! Descend into the brain and body of every human being on Earth this moment and all who come here in the future! Take possession of that which is already Yours, and once again compel everything in mankind and its outer activity to come into Divine Order through Divine Love and be eternally sustained!

We thank Thee Thou dost always answer our every Call.

✧ 52 ✧

LEGAL DECREE

"MIGHTY I AM PRESENCE," GREAT HOST OF ASCENDED MASTERS AND GREAT COSMIC BEINGS! Come forth in Your Full Cosmic Power and Authority of the Unfed Flame, the "Three times Three," the Cosmic Light, and the Blue Lightning of Divine Love! Blast this instant by the Power of the Blue Ray all legal procedure from existence within the United States of America and throughout the world, that is not the Eternal Divine Law of Right and Justice of the "Mighty I AM Presence" and the Ascended Masters for every human being on Earth forever! Annihilate all that does not guarantee and give Divine Justice to every human being on Earth forever! Blast the cause and effect of all that binds humanity by wrong legal activity, and replace it by the Ascended Masters' Eternal Divine

Justice to all forever! Replace all legal procedure throughout the world with the Ascended Masters' Eternal Divine Law of the "Mighty I AM Presence" that gives Divine Justice to every human being on Earth forever! We thank Thee Thou dost always answer our every Call instantly forever!

✧ 53 ✧
LIGHT

"MIGHTY INFINITE I AM PRESENCE," GREAT HOST OF ASCENDED MASTERS, MIGHTY LEGIONS OF LIGHT, GREAT ANGELIC HOST, GREAT COSMIC BEINGS, AND GREAT COSMIC LIGHT!

In the Mightiest Victory of Love that Earth has ever known, blaze through us Thy Cosmic Light; Thy Light! Light! Light! Thy Limitless, Shadowless Light! the Mighty Eternal "Light of God that Never Fails," in Its most Instantaneous, Dynamic Action. Sweep It through us with the Onrush of a Mighty Torrent! Carry into the sea of oblivion every limitation of the children of Earth.

"I AM" a Child of the Light! I love the Light! I live in the Light! I serve the Light! I bless the Light! I worship the Light! I am eternally supplied by the Light! protected by the Light! healed by the Light and forever sustained by the Light; and "I AM" the Limitless Outpouring of all Light, until Its Radiance comes through my flesh, illumines everything I contact, and keeps It eternally sustained!

"Mighty I AM Presence," we charge all our music and Decrees with Saint Germain, Jesus, Nada, and the Divine Director's Ascended Master Consciousness, Instantaneous Activity and Fulfillment of our every Conscious Command of the "I AM," the Supreme Source of all Light.

We thank Thee Thou dost always answer our every Call instantly.

✧ 54 ✧

MINING

"MIGHTY INFINITE I AM PRESENCE," GREAT HOST OF ASCENDED MASTERS, MIGHTY LEGIONS OF LIGHT, GREAT ANGELIC HOST, GREAT GUARDIANS OF THE HEIGHTS, AND GREAT COSMIC BEINGS! COME FORTH BY THE POWER OF THE UNFED FLAME, THE "THREE

TIMES THREE" AND THE COSMIC LIGHT!

Blast from existence forever all that interferes with perfect mining activities everywhere! Annihilate all such causes and effects from existence forever! Seize, bind, hold inactive, and remove from the Earth and its atmosphere all discarnate entities within and around all mines and all that is connected with them in any way! Replace them by the Guardian Angels of the Blue Lightning of Divine Love! Release from every mine throughout the world all the Mighty Gifts of the "I AM Presence" from those channels! See that all is used in the Service of the Light for the Eternal Blessing of mankind!

Charge forth Ascended Master Protection, Consciousness, Management, and Activity everywhere throughout America–yes! the Americas! in these activities, and throughout the world! Open up those wonderful resources and release the new supply of gold and all forms of wealth for the incoming Golden Age! See that everything within those channels is used constructively and to expand Ascended Master Perfection everywhere through all forever!

Charge the minds and bodies of all who are connected with those activities with Ascended Master Consciousness, Substance, and the Cosmic Light! Show them the perfect thing to do at *all* times, and see that they *do it perfectly*! Give all such activities the Invincible Protection of the Cosmic Light, the Unfed Flame and the Ascended Masters, by the Power of the "Three times Three."

I have spoken in the Name of the "Mighty I AM Presence," and what I have decreed shall come to pass now through Divine Love, eternally sustained, and I thank Thee Thou dost always answer our every Call!

✧ 55 ✧

MUSIC AND DANCING

"MIGHTY I AM PRESENCE," GREAT HOST OF ASCENDED MASTERS, MIGHTY LEGIONS OF LIGHT, GREAT ANGELIC HOST, GREAT COSMIC BEINGS, AND ESPECIALLY ALL WHO PRODUCE AND GOVERN THE MUSIC OF THE SPHERES!

Sweep Your Violet Consuming Flame of Divine Love, Purity, and Perfection through all so-called musical and dance activities of mankind everywhere on Earth! Annihilate all destructive qualities, rhythm and combinations, and blast their cause and effect from existence within mankind, the Earth and its atmosphere forever! Replace such activities with the Full Eternal Perfection of the Music of the Spheres!

Great Celestial Choir and all Beings from the Temples of Light, Music and Healing, the Glorious Tenor from Saint Germain's Retreat, Mrs. Rayborn, and all those particularly concerned with the Outpouring and Service of Music! Charge all our Music with Ascended Master Perfection! Sing with and through us! Let us hear You in the physical octave! Charge all the "I AM" Students with the Ascended Masters' Golden Voice in both speech and song! Amplify our Music without limit, and charge it with Saint Germain, Jesus, Nada, and the Divine Director's Ascended Master Consciousness of the "Mighty I AM Presence"! Charge it forth with such Almighty Illumining Power and Activity into the brain and body of every human being on Earth, that no human creation can longer resist Its Mighty Victory and Perfection! Amplify our gratitude and adoration with the Light and Love as of a Thousand Suns! Blaze It throughout the Earth, and keep our Songs and Music eternally active, until every human being is Free!

✧ 56 ✧

OPERA, DRAMA, MUSIC, AND ART

"MIGHTY I AM PRESENCE," GREAT HOST OF ASCENDED MASTERS, MIGHTY LEGIONS OF LIGHT, GREAT ANGELIC HOST, GREAT COSMIC BEINGS, AND GREAT COSMIC LIGHT! Come forth everywhere in the channels of opera, drama, music, and art! Compel every destructive, imperfect quality and activity within those channels to annihilate itself and its own cause and effect! Then release into and through those channels the magnificent Ascended Master Cosmic Opera, Drama, Music, and Art to come forth! Expand the Perfection of the "Mighty I AM Presence" and the Ascended Masters everywhere into the Life and activity of all humanity, and keep It forever sustained! Let this come forth *now* with the speed of thought to bless all with the greatest joy possible!

We thank Thee Thou dost always answer our every Call!

✧ 57 ✧

OBEDIENCE TO DIVINE PLAN FOR PERFECTING AMERICA

"MIGHTY I AM PRESENCE," GREAT HOST OF ASCENDED MASTERS, GREAT COSMIC BEINGS, AND LORDS OF THE FLAME FROM VENUS!

In Thy Full Authority of the Great Cosmic Law, project the Great Cosmic Light with Irresistible Force throughout the government of the United States of America, and hold all individuals true to their oath of office, and obedient to the Divine Plan of the Great Cosmic Beings for the *perfecting of America*, the government, and Her people! Come forth! Take possession of all governmental offices, hold Your Dominion and Divine Justice everywhere within our government forever! We thank Thee Thou dost always answer our every Call, and it is eternally sustained and ever-expanding!

✧ 58 ✧

ORGAN

"MIGHTY I AM PRESENCE" AND GREAT HOST OF ASCENDED MASTERS!

Give us the Perfect Organ as a Glad-free Gift of Love for our "I AM" Reading Room and Classes to be used in our Group Meetings; that we may more efficiently serve the Light in music and song. We thank Thee it is done!

✧ 59 ✧

PERFECTION IN THE "I AM" WORK

"MIGHTY I AM PRESENCE," GREAT HOST OF ASCENDED MASTERS, MIGHTY LEGIONS OF LIGHT, GREAT ANGELIC HOST, GREAT COSMIC BEINGS, LORDS OF THE FLAME FROM VENUS, GREAT GOD TABOR, MIGHTY GOD OF NATURE, GREAT INTELLIGENCES IN CHARGE OF THE AIR, WATER, EARTH, AND FIRE ELEMENTS!

Come forth in Your Full Cosmic Authority! By the Power of the Unfed Flame the "Three times Three," and the Great Cosmic Light.

Blaze forth eternally Your Full Perfection everywhere in this Work of the "Mighty I AM Presence" brought forth by Saint Germain! See that the Messengers and Students always have clear, calm, comfortable, perfect weather wherever they are! particularly at all Classes, and traveling to and from all Classes! See that every person, place, condition, and thing in this Activity is *invincibly protected at all times*, eternally sustained, and supplied with ten times the money and every good thing they require–perfect hotel accommodations, perfect food, perfect travelling conditions, whether by land, water, or air; and that all is used forever in the Service of the Ascended Masters. We thank Thee, it is always done!

✧ 60 ✧

PROTECTION FROM HUMAN SUGGESTION

"MIGHTY I AM PRESENCE"! Don't let any person, place, condition or thing dare influence me but Your and the Ascended Masters' Perfection. "Mighty I AM," see that I do not take on suggestions from any person, place, condition or thing, but You and Your Perfection and that of the Ascended Masters–forever!

✧ 61 ✧

PROTECT AMERICA FROM WAR

"MIGHTY I AM PRESENCE," GREAT HOST OF ASCENDED MASTERS, MIGHTY LEGIONS OF LIGHT, GREAT ANGELIC HOST, GREAT COSMIC BEINGS, GREAT COSMIC LIGHT!

Come forth this instant in Thy Full Cosmic Power and Authority–in Thy Full Cosmic Activity of the Blue Lightning–the Blue Lightning of Divine Love–fill and surround the United States of America with Thy Mighty Invincible Protection forever! In the Name of the "I AM Presence," we, the Children of the Light, command and decree that there shall not be war in nor with America, or the Americas!

Mighty Arcturus, Great Cyclopea, Mighty Silent Watcher, Great God Meru, and Mighty God Tabor, Saint Germain, Jesus, Nada and the Divine Director! Send those Angels of Blue Lightning of whom You are the Directors, everywhere within the borders of the Americas! Loose whatever Action of "the Light of God that never fails" which is necessary to blast the cause and effect of all suggestion or activity of war! War *shall not* manifest again on Earth! Do Thou O "Infinite I AM Presence," take up this Decree! Charge It with the Blue Lightning of Divine Love, and let It go everywhere throughout the Earth! until it absolutely neutralizes all consciousness and activity of war forever! "The Light of God Never Fails," and America is that Light!

In the Name of the "Mighty I AM Presence," by the Power of the Unfed Flame, the "Three times Three," and the Cosmic Light! Send Thy Angels of Invincible Protection to the Children of Light, and take them forward to Victory this instant! I have spoken in the Name of the Infinite "I AM Presence," and the Mighty Host of Ascended Masters, the Legions of Light, the Great Angelic Host, and Cosmic Beings! Do Thou fulfill this Decree *now* and forever, and we thank Thee.

✧ 62 ✧

PROTECTING AMERICA'S ATMOSPHERE

A

Great Divine Director's Request: Never miss a day, and before you retire at night, say to all human creation:

IN THE NAME OF MY "MIGHTY I AM PRESENCE" AND THE POWER OF THE ASCENDED MASTERS!

I say to all human creation: *you have no power*! "Mighty I AM Presence" and Great Cosmic Light, project Thy Mighty Light Rays in and through the Earth, establishing Thy Currents throughout the atmosphere of Earth; and cause all destructive qualities and their activities to cease to exist.

Then We will do the rest.

B

"MIGHTY I AM PRESENCE," GREAT HOST OF ASCENDED MASTERS, GREAT ANGELIC HOST, MIGHTY LEGIONS OF LIGHT, GREAT COSMIC BEINGS, AND GREAT COSMIC LIGHT!

Come forth at once in Your Full Power of the Unfed Flame, the "Three times Three" and the Cosmic Light! Charge and qualify all the atmosphere within, around, and above the Americas with the Blue Lightning of the Ascended Masters' Divine Love, Light Substance and Power. Fill it so full of this Blazing Presence that It instantly repels all activities unlike Itself–all that does not have constructive intent and activity to the Americas! Give the Americas this Mighty Invincible Protection now and forever without limit, and ever expand Thy Almighty Victories of the "Light of God that never fails." We thank Thee Thou dost always answer our every Call, and this is instantly and infinitely manifest, eternally sustained and ever-expanding.

✧ 63 ✧

PERFECT WEATHER CONDITIONS AND CROPS

"MIGHTY I AM PRESENCE," GREAT HOST OF ASCENDED MASTERS, MIGHTY COSMIC BEINGS, GREAT COSMIC LIGHT, MIGHTY GOD OF NATURE, AND THE GREAT BEINGS WHO CONTROL THE ACTION OF THE ELEMENTS!

Come forth everywhere within our Beloved United States of America and the Americas! Stand guard over all activities of Nature and the Elements within our borders forever! Blast the cause and effect of all drought, floods, storms, and destructive activities of the elements in every way! Bring *perfect balance everywhere,* and so bless Nature with Thy Ascended Master Purity, Light and Love that the most lavish production and Ascended Master Miracles, Blessings, and Perfection the Earth has ever known shall come forth everywhere to bless all–*now*–and forever! Blast all human consciousness and its cause and effect that dares to attempt to destroy crops or nature's production in order to control prices or for any reason whatever! Annihilate the cause and effect of that viciousness from the planet forever! In the Name of the "Mighty I AM Presence," by the Power of the Unfed Flame, the "Three times Three," and the Cosmic Light, such viciousness shall annihilate itself from this Earth and its people, and be replaced by Ascended Master Intelligence, Love, Light, Wisdom, and Power in Perfect Balance and Control throughout America and the world forever! Great Beings of Light! Charge this Decree–*this Fiat*–forth with whatever Power is necessary to bring It to pass instantly, infinitely and eternally for the Blessing of all, and keep it forever expanding.

✧ 64 ✧

PRESS

"MIGHTY I AM PRESENCE," GREAT HOST OF ASCENDED MASTERS, GREAT COSMIC BEINGS AND GREAT COSMIC LIGHT!

Come forth in Your Cosmic Authority! By the Power of the Unfed Flame, the "Three times Three," and the Great Cosmic Light! Prevent the *press, reporters*, and all outer channels of activity from making any false statements about this Work of Saint Germain's Instruction of the "Mighty I AM Presence" or casting discredit upon It in any way! *Silence* everything of that kind throughout the world forever! See that the whole world stands back of this Glorious Work and gives It the recognition, honor, and credit that is due the Great Blessed Presence of Saint Germain and the other Ascended Masters who have brought It forth! Bless and charge the Press and all channels of information and communication with Ascended Master Consciousness, Obedience and Perfection in all their activities forever, and so control them that they serve only "the Light of God that never fails." Drench them with the Limitless Blessings of the Ascended Masters forever. We thank Thee Thou dost always answer our every Call!

✧ 65 ✧

POLICEMEN, FIREMEN, AVIATORS, PUBLIC SERVANTS

"MIGHTY I AM PRESENCE," GREAT HOST OF ASCENDED MASTERS, MIGHTY LEGIONS OF LIGHT, GREAT ANGELIC HOST, GREAT COSMIC BEINGS AND GREAT COSMIC LIGHT!

Blaze forth Thy Almighty, Invincible, Eternal Protection, Ascended Master Consciousness and Substance in, through, and around every policeman, fireman, aviator, postal employee, school teacher, governmental official, doctor, nurse, and public servant! See that they always maintain Protection, Peace, Order, and Divine Justice, and serve "the Light of God that never fails"–and blaze around them the Invincible Protection of that Light. We thank Thee it is done, eternally sustained and ever-expanding.

✧ 66 ✧

PRECIPITATED BUILDINGS

"MIGHTY I AM PRESENCE," GREAT HOST OF ASCENDED MASTERS, MIGHTY LEGIONS OF LIGHT, GREAT ANGELIC HOST, GREAT GODS OF THE MOUNTAINS, GREAT COSMIC BEINGS, LORDS OF THE FLAME FROM VENUS, AND THE SEVEN GREAT ELOHIM OF CREATION!

Come forth in Your full Cosmic Authority! By the Power of the Unfed Flame, the "Three times Three," and the Great Cosmic Light! precipitate *Magnificent, Perfect, Imperishable Buildings,* Temples of Light of the "Mighty I AM Presence" and Ascended Masters, into which the Students under this Radiation can come together and call forth the Ascended Master Activity of the "Mighty I AM Presence" for the Freedom, Perfection and Ascension of all mankind, and the Illumination of the Earth! Charge forth through these Temples such Glory, Perfection, and Love from the Ascended Masters and Angelic Host, as the Earth has never before known in any age! Release ten times the money and all forms of supply that may be necessary, with Invincible Protection, for their Perfect Maintenance! Through these Temples bring forth Thy Perfection in every person, place, condition, and thing on this planet!

Keep It expanding the Victory, Beauty, Freedom, and Glory of the "Mighty I AM Presence" forever!

Great Builders of the Cosmic Perfection! In the Fullness of Thy Love, lower into the physical octave of our Earth these Mighty, Perfect Temples which are waiting to be used. See that the "I AM" Students fulfill all conditions which are required to enable this to be done; that the world may see the Ascended Masters' Glory releasing Its Mighty Truth and Perfection, give Eternal Obedience to the "Mighty I AM Presence," and be forever Free!

We Thank Thee Thou dost always answer our every Call! Keep it eternally sustained and ever-expanding.

✧ 67 ✧

PENAL INSTITUTIONS, ASYLUMS, COURTS, POLICEMEN

"MIGHTY INFINITE I AM PRESENCE," GREAT HOST OF ASCENDED MASTERS, GREAT COSMIC BEINGS, GREAT LORDS OF THE FLAME FROM VENUS, MIGHTY ANGELS OF THE VIOLET AND BLUE LIGHTNING OF DIVINE LOVE, AND THOSE

WHO WIELD THE SWORD OF BLUE FLAME OF DIVINE LOVE!

Come forth this very instant in and around every Student of the "I AM" and all who sincerely seek the Light throughout the Earth; into all penal institutions, hospitals and insane asylums; all courts of Law, into all police activities! Seize, bind, hold inactive, and remove every discarnate entity in and around these special activities! Hold them bound and inactive in the Octave of Light until they willingly surrender everything to the Light, and in humble, grateful, loving, adoring, eternal obedience, serve that Light forever and gain their Freedom! Replace all such entities with the Substance from the Ascended Masters' Octave of Life, with Ascended Master Consciousness and Activity, with the Ascended Masters' Visible, Tangible, Living, Breathing Presence, and that of the Angelic Host; that the Earth may once again be peopled with Divine Beings, and mankind be released into its own Divine Way of Life.

Come forth, O Thou Mighty Cosmic Light! Seize, bind, hold inactive forever the animal within every human body on Earth! Blaze through it your Sword of Blue Flame of the Consuming Power of Divine Love, and once and forever, "Mighty I AM Presence" of every human being on Earth, come forth and take possession of your own physical personalities. Claim everybody and everything into the Service of the Light. Hold everyone's attention on the "Mighty I AM Presence" and the Perfection of the Ascended Masters! Once again humanity *shall* manifest the Perfection which Thou art, and forever sustain It through Thy Mighty Love and Light. We thank Thee, Thou dost always answer our every Call, instantly, infinitely, eternally, and ever-expanding!

✧ 68 ✧
PROTECTION

"MIGHTY I AM PRESENCE"! Don't let any feeling register in me and my world but the Heart of Your Love. Protect my feelings by Your Invincible Wall of Light forever!

✧ 69 ✧

RADIO BROADCASTING STATION TELEVISION, MOVIES, EDUCATION HEALING

THOU "MIGHTY INFINITE I AM PRESENCE," GREAT HOST OF ASCENDED MASTERS, MIGHTY LEGIONS OF LIGHT, GREAT ANGELIC HOST, GREAT COSMIC BEINGS, LORDS OF THE FLAME FROM VENUS, AND MIGHTY ELOHIM OF CREATION!

Come forth in Your Cosmic Power and Authority of the Eternal Unfed Flame of Divine Love, the "Three times Three" and the Cosmic Light! Release into our use at once as Your Glad-free Gift of Love, our own Radio Broadcasting Station with a national and world hookup, eternally sustained. Blaze forth into the atmosphere of Earth this Ascended Master Instruction of the "Mighty I AM Presence" to reach everyone within the Americas, and then expand It throughout the Earth for the Freedom of all!

Send Your and our Blessing into all radio activity! Purify it, illumine it, and bring forth such Perfection as has never before been experienced on Earth in all those channels! Release into our use in the outer world right now the Perfect Radio and Television apparatus which is now in the Ascended Masters'

Retreats! Let this Great Perfection for all come forth at once to release the Fullness of Its Blessing everywhere! Make every human being on Earth realize that no one can lose anything but his limitation and distress in accepting this Mighty Ascended Master Knowledge of the "Mighty I AM Presence" in using It to call forth these wonderful, new and perfect inventions to bless all mankind!

We also expand and command this Blessing and Invincible Ascended Master Protection to go forth and envelop everything in aviation, transportation, communication, public utilities, and all channels serving the necessities of Life to mankind. We charge forth the same Perfection into all activities of the press, movies, education, and healing; that the Mightiest Release possible *shall* go forth *now* to bless and perfect every activity for humanity, bring such joy and miraculous action on Earth, that all mankind will know of and accept this Divine Way, the Natural Way to live Life, and give obedience forever to the "I AM Presence."

Charge all these channels with Ascended Master Consciousness, and release through them the Ascended Masters' Mighty Blessing for mankind, which must come forth now! Make them all channels of Eternal Truth, Blessing, and Service to mankind, and nothing else! Place an Ascended Master in charge of each one of these activities, and fulfill the Divine

Plan for America and the Earth right now!

"The Light of God Never Fails!" "The Light of God Never Fails!" "The Light of God Never Fails!" America is drenched with that Ascended Master Substance and is forever sustained by the "Mighty I AM Presence" and Ascended Masters, as a Holy Grail of Their Almighty Consciousness and Perfection to the Earth forever! We thank Thee for this accomplishment! Release it to every human being on Earth in physical manifestation, eternally sustained and ever-expanding!

America, we love you! America, we love you! America, we love you with a Love unspeakable! We seal you within the Presence of the Diamond Heart.

✧ 70 ✧

RELEASE FROM HYPNOTIC DOMINATION

"MIGHTY I AM PRESENCE," GREAT HOST OF ASCENDED MASTERS, MIGHTY LEGIONS OF LIGHT, MIGHTY LORDS OF THE FLAME FROM VENUS, GREAT COSMIC BEINGS, AND GREAT COSMIC LIGHT!

Sweep Your Violet Consuming Flame through the consciousness of mankind, the Earth and its atmosphere everywhere! Annihilate all human suggestion and hypnotic domination from the face of the Earth forever! Give each individual his complete and Eternal Freedom! See that each thinks and feels only the Victory of his "Presence"! Insulate every human being within the Magic Electronic Tube of Ascended Master Light Substance which cuts him free forever from all qualities but the Perfection of his "Mighty I AM Presence" and the Ascended Masters!

Lift blessed, beloved humanity into the full conscious acceptance of the "I AM Presence," and hold every human being within the Victory of "the Light of God that never fails." Annihilate everything that dares to interfere with the Expansion of the Light of any human being on the Earth! Blast all such causes and effects from existence forever! Seize the attention of the mind, body, being and world of every human being on Earth. Seize the vision, sight, and hearing of every human being, and anchor it wholly on his own "I AM Presence," the very Source of his own Life. Cut all mankind free from the magnetic pull of Earth, the things of Earth and all human creation, that everyone may unmistakably feel his own Freedom and Dominion and keep it forever sustained.

We say to blessed humanity everywhere! Awake! awake! awake! to this Full Conscious Ascended Master Knowledge of your own "I AM Presence." Be 100%

loyal to yourself, the Ascended Master Perfection of the Light! Reach up and take your Scepter of Dominion, produce Perfection and hold It forever! The Victory of the ages is at hand! The Victory of the Light is at hand–"The Light of God That Never Fails," and is eternally sustained!

Blessed, beloved humanity, our Love and our Light of the "Mighty I AM Presence" is great enough to lift you into the Light once again, and so shall you be Free! We thank Thee, "Mighty I AM Presence," Thou dost always answer our every Call, instantly, infinitely, and eternally!

✧ 71 ✧

REMOVAL OF ENTITIES–CARNATE AND DISCARNATE

"MIGHTY I AM PRESENCE," GREAT HOST OF ASCENDED MASTERS, MIGHTY LEGIONS OF LIGHT, GREAT ANGELIC HOST, GREAT COSMIC BEINGS AND GREAT COSMIC LIGHT!

Blaze forth Your Limitless Power of the Blue Ray, the Blue Lightning and Sword of Blue Flame of Divine Love! Seize, bind, hold inactive and remove from within and around every human being, the Earth and its atmosphere, every discarnate entity! Take them *all* from this planet instantly, and to the Octave of Light! Hold them there bound and inactive until they surrender everything to the Light, and serve It eternally in humble, grateful, loving, adoring obedience, and gain their Freedom!

Blast from existence instantly all humanly-created entities, their cause and effect within and around every human body, the Earth and its atmosphere forever! Replace all entities by the Ascended Masters' Consciousness, Light Substance, Purity, Invincible Protection, Perfection and Visible, Tangible, Living, Breathing Presence, eternally sustained! Bring this to pass with the speed and Power of the Blue Lightning of Divine Love! Give blessed humanity this complete release *now*, and keep it forever sustained! We thank Thee Thou dost always answer our every Call instantly, infinitely, and eternally!

✧ 72 ✧

RELEASE ANIMAL LIFE

O "INFINITE MIGHTY I AM PRESENCE," GREAT HOST OF ASCENDED MASTERS AND GREAT COSMIC BEINGS!

In the Limitless Cosmic Light of the Unfed Flame in Its most Dynamic Irresistible Activity! come forth and charge through us Thy Mighty Ascended Master Victory of the Light everywhere we move, and to all to which our thought is directed. Come forth in Thy Cosmic Action of the Sword of Blue Flame, and cut to pieces everything that binds mankind to discordant activity. Seize, bind and hold inactive every person, place, condition or thing that will not serve the Light, and compel them to manifest Perfection and Harmony.

Release the life in all animal forms on this planet into their own right channels of activity, love, beauty, harmony and Perfection! See that none of Life ever again has to function in forms that are less than the Perfection of the Ascended Masters. Release all life in animal form into that Realm of Beauty and Perfection where it really belongs! Replace all animal creations by the Purity, Glory, Majesty, Beauty, Freedom, Victory, and the Perfection of the Ascended Masters.

In the name of the "Infinite I AM Presence" I have spoken, and so shall it manifest now and forever! Great Beings of Light throughout Infinity, release whatever Power is necessary to fulfill our Decree in physical manifestation on Earth—*now*!

We thank Thee Thou dost always answer our Call.

✧ 73 ✧

RENUNCIATION FOR ALL MANKIND

ALL HAS COME FORTH FROM THE LIGHT! ALL BELONGS TO THE LIGHT! ALL OUGHT TO BE IN THE SERVICE OF THE LIGHT! Therefore, we make the renunciation for all mankind, and offer the Earth and all on this planet once again unto the Light for their Eternal Perfection

"Mighty I AM Presence," Great Host of Ascended Masters, Mighty Legions of Light, Great Angelic Host, Great Cosmic Beings, and Great Cosmic Light! We, as atoms in the body of humanity, offer once again unto the Light, the Earth, mankind, and all upon this planet forever! ACCEPT THEM! HOLD THEM! RAISE THEM! INTO THE FULL PERFECTION OF THE ASCENDED MASTERS' OCTAVE OF

LIGHT. KEEP IT SUSTAINED IN EVER-EXPANDING GLORY AND PERFECTION OF ETERNAL LIGHT!

✧ 74 ✧

READING ROOMS, STUDY GROUPS, ETC.

"MIGHTY I AM PRESENCE," GREAT HOST OF ASCENDED MASTERS, MIGHTY LEGIONS OF LIGHT, GREAT ANGELIC HOST, GREAT COSMIC BEINGS, AND GREAT COSMIC LIGHT!

Reach out Your Hands and bring into our "I AM" Reading Rooms, Study Groups, Schools, and Classes all who sincerely seek the Light! Keep out *all* others! Make each of these Activities such a gigantic Pillar of the Unfed Flame in Its Almighty Activity, that all who contact them will be instantly set Free in every way, and then render that Service to the Light and America which sets others Free also! Supply each one of these activities with ten times more than they need of every good thing, money included, and see that all is used in the Service of the Light to expand! expand! and again expand! this Work without limit until all mankind is

Free. We thank Thee Thou dost always answer our every Call instantly, and it is eternally sustained and ever-expanding!

✧ 75 ✧

RACIAL DISTINCTIONS

MIGHTY BEINGS OF LIGHT WHOSE PROVINCE IT IS TO RENDER THIS SERVICE!

Come forth in Your Cosmic Action and do this for mankind *now*! We make the Call in the Name of the "I AM Presence," and we give praise and thanks that You do answer us now and forever! Wipe out from all mankind all racial distinctions and characteristics of every sort! Let *every* race return to the Ascended Master Divine Pattern, Appearance, Characteristics, Purity, and Activity for all, and once again make the whole human race outpicture the Perfection of the Ascended Masters, thereafter be a credit to their Source, and blaze Perfection everywhere!

✧ 76 ✧

SUPPLY

"MIGHTY INFINITE I AM PRESENCE," GREAT HOST OF ASCENDED MASTERS, MIGHTY LORD THE MAHA CHOHAN, AND BLESSED, BELOVED SANAT KUMARA!

By the Power of Thy Mighty Love, wield Thy Sword of Blue Flame and project the Lightning of Thy Love into the mass entity of mankind that has created the feeling and lack of money or any good thing! Blast that consciousness from humanity forever! Annihilate its cause and effect this moment, and replace it by the Limitless Consciousness and Lavish Supply from the Ascended Masters' Octave of Life! Charge all with the Ascended Masters' Consciousness of the Inexhaustible Supply and the physical manifestation of every good thing by the Power of Divine Love, released into the physical use of humanity everywhere, this instant and forever! See that mankind accepts this in its *feelings* and goes forward Eternally Free, supplied with ten times more than it needs of every good thing! See that all is used forever in the Service of the Light!

See that everyone who serves the Light is forever Invincibly Protected and never lacks for any good thing! In the Name of the "I AM Presence," I have spoken, and so shall it be released to the children of Earth! We thank Thee Thou Great Host of Light for Thy Ascended Masters' Consciousness, Instantaneous Activity and Fulfillment of this our Decree for the Freedom of all, and we thank Thee it is eternally sustained and ever-expanding!

✧ 77 ✧

STRIKE AGITATORS

"MIGHTY I AM PRESENCE," GREAT HOST OF ASCENDED MASTERS, GREAT COSMIC BEINGS AND GREAT COSMIC LIGHT!

Seize, bind, hold inactive and remove completely from the United States of America and the Americas, all strike agitators! Take them where they cannot create further disturbance or interfere with the Peace, Perfect Balance, Perfection and Expansion of "the Light of God that never fails," coming forth everywhere in the industrial and commercial activity of all in the Americas! Annihilate all strike agitation from the face of the Earth, and blast its cause and effect from the memory of mankind forever! We thank Thee Thou dost always answer our every Call instantly, infinitely, and eternally!

Seize, bind, and make helpless every destructive force that attempts such an action! Hold them bound and inactive! Withdraw and withhold all energy, money, power, influence and supply of every kind from every channel that attempts such a thing! Replace them instantly by the Ascended Masters' actual Presence, Consciousness, Substance, Power and Activity! Take complete possession of all strike conditions and replace them by Ascended Master Perfection and Divine Justice instantly manifest, and eternally sustained! All disturbing activities shall cease from the experience of mankind this instant, and once again the Great Ascended Host of Light shall walk and talk with the blessed people of Earth face to face, in their Tangible Bodies, and mankind comrade with the Angels.

See that every word we have spoken this day is fulfilled instantly by the Power of the Ascended Masters' Light and Love, and is eternally sustained. We thank Thee Thou dost always answer our every Call!

✧ 78 ✧

SAINT GERMAIN PRESS
"VOICE OF THE I AM"

"MIGHTY INFINITE I AM PRESENCE," GREAT HOST OF ASCENDED MASTERS, MIGHTY LEGIONS OF LIGHT, GREAT ANGELIC HOST, GREAT COSMIC BEINGS AND GREAT COSMIC LIGHT!

Come forth in Your combined Power of Love, Light and constant Blessing to the children of Earth! Bless and protect the Saint Germain Press, Class Work, Lectures, the periodical known as the *"Voice of the I AM,"* and all their activities forever! Charge them with such amazing Ascended Master Consciousness, Management and Perfection that they cover the Earth with this Mighty Ascended Master Instruction of the "I AM"! See that every human being on the Earth seeks and receives these marvelous books and magazines! Draw the attention of all on this planet to the "Mighty I AM Presence," and the Ascended Masters, and set them Free forever!

Charge everything concerning these publications and activities with the Almighty Perfection of the Ascended Masters, ten times more of every good thing than they can possibly need, as a Glad-free Gift of Love from the Presence! See that all is used only in the

Service of the Light! Expand through these channels such Limitless Light and Blessings from the Great Host of Ascended Masters, that the Earth shall blaze with Their Glory, and every human being become Free! Bring this to pass instantly and infinitely; keep it eternally sustained and ever-expanding!

✧ 79 ✧

SCHOOLS

"MIGHTY I AM PRESENCE," GREAT HOST OF ASCENDED MASTERS, MIGHTY LEGIONS OF LIGHT, GREAT ANGELIC HOST AND GREAT COSMIC BEINGS!

Come forth in Your Cosmic Power and Authority of the Unfed Flame, the "Three times Three" and the Cosmic Light! Establish the *New Schools* of the *Ascended Masters' Teaching* for the *New Cycle*! Reach out Your Hands and bring into them all Young America, and through them release the Ascended Masters' Full Truth and Law! Bring forth the *Perfect Method of Teaching* in every channel, and make all activities of education Supreme Ascended Master Happiness for both teachers and students! Release the *Mighty Ascended Masters' Joy of Life* in every such activity, and produce the *Mighty Perfection* which will enable Victory to come through everywhere instantly, infinitely, eternally sustained and ever-expanding.

✧ 80 ✧

SUPPLY TO ALL UNDER THIS RADIATION

"MIGHTY I AM PRESENCE," GREAT HOST OF ASCENDED MASTERS, MIGHTY LEGIONS OF LIGHT, GREAT ANGELIC HOST, GREAT COSMIC BEINGS, GREAT COSMIC LIGHT AND MIGHTY ELOHIM OF CREATION!

Release this instant into the hands and use of everyone under this Radiation and to all who seek sincerely the Light throughout the world, Thy Inexhaustible, Ever-expanding Supply of every good thing forever, as Your Glad-free Gift of Love! See that no one under this Radiation lacks for any good thing, but make all crystal clear channels for the continuous Outpouring of Thy Limitless Blessings to all forever! Keep this eternally sustained and ever-expanding!

✧ 81 ✧

SIGHT AND HEARING

"MIGHTY BLESSED I AM PRESENCE," GREAT HOST OF ASCENDED MASTERS, MIGHTY LEGIONS OF LIGHT, GREAT ANGELIC HOST, GREAT COSMIC BEINGS!

Come forth in Your Limitless Power of the Unfed Flame, the "Three times Three" and the Cosmic Light, the Blue Ray and the Sword of Blue Flame of Divine Love! Consume everything within and around mankind, the Earth and its atmosphere that limits blessed humanity's sight and hearing! Beloved Cyclopea, blaze forth Your Power of the All-Seeing Eye of God, consume from the vision of mankind all interference with the seeing of Thy Full Perfection everywhere! Charge the physical eyes of every human being on Earth with Thy Mighty Power of *Perfect Sight*! Let them see their own "I AM Presence" face to face; see all things, see through all things perfectly, and see Perfection everywhere! Charge humanity with Thy Perfect Vision, and blast all that dares to interfere with Its Mighty Blessing to all forever! Charge the ears of mankind with Thy *Perfect Hearing*, and make it impossible for anyone to hear anything but the Voice of his own "I AM Presence" and the Eternal Truth of the Ascended

Masters, that each human being may know the Eternal Source of his own Life, hear Its Voice distinctly, obey Its Commands, and come once again into Freedom!

Annihilate the cause and effect within the thoughts and feelings of mankind, the Earth and its atmosphere that try to interfere with humanity's *Perfect Sight and Hearing*! Blast all that produced these conditions in the past or present! Release the Cosmic Action of the Violet Consuming Flame! Seal every human being on Earth now within a Gigantic Pillar of the Ascended Masters Violet Consuming Flame, the Flame of Divine Love! Let It consume all unlike Itself! Keep It sustained until the moment of their Ascension, and release through the "I AM" Students the Cosmic Light as of a Thousand Suns to bring Perfection to blessed humanity everywhere, through the Power of Love and Light–Irresistible, Invincible, Almighty, Eternal! With the speed of thought bring forth this Perfection to mankind that all may accept the Presence of the "I AM" and have their release quickly. We Thank Thee Thou dost always answer our every Call instantly, infinitely and eternally!

✧ 82 ✧

SERUMS

"MIGHTY I AM PRESENCE," GREAT HOST OF ASCENDED MASTERS, MIGHTY LEGIONS OF LIGHT, GREAT ANGELIC HOST, GREAT COSMIC BEINGS, GREAT COSMIC LIGHT, LORDS OF THE FLAME FROM VENUS, ASTREA, OROMASIS AND THE ARCHANGEL MICHAEL!

Come forth in Your *Limitless Cosmic Power of the Sword of Blue Flame of Divine Love* and the *Violet Consuming Flame*! Compel all activity and use of serums to annihilate itself, its cause and effect from mankind, the Earth and its atmosphere *now!* Blast all such vicious concepts and activities from human experience forever! Replace them by the *Ascended Masters' Wisdom and Instantaneous Healing Power of the Light Rays!* Release to and through all avenues of healing the *Pure, True, Ascended Master Power* to produce *Perfection* for all everywhere forever! We thank Thee Thou dost answer our every Call instantly, infinitely, and eternally!

✧ 83 ✧

STRIKES

"MIGHTY INFINITE I AM PRESENCE," GREAT HOST OF ASCENDED MASTERS, GREAT COSMIC BEINGS!

Come forth in the Full Cosmic Power of the Unfed Flame, the "Three times Three" and the Great Cosmic Light! Blast all strikes and their cause and effect from existence forever within the borders of the United States of America and the world! See that Divine Justice is rendered everywhere to both so-called labor and capital. Bring about perfect, loving cooperation in all business activities, that the Limitless Supply of every good thing may now come forth to bless all! Compel everyone to render Divine Justice to both capital and labor! Make it impossible for another strike to ever occur again within the borders of our Beloved America or anywhere among mankind! Great Host of Ascended Masters and Great Cosmic Beings! Send the Angels of Blue Lightning of Divine Love and the Sword of Blue Flame of Divine Love, to drive into the cause and effect of all strikes and all those which are being contemplated! Loose that Activity this very instant with the Power of Ten Thousand Suns! to consume forever every such attempt throughout the Earth, and especially within the United States of America!

✧ 84 ✧
TIME

"MIGHTY I AM PRESENCE," GREAT HOST OF ASCENDED MASTERS, MIGHTY LEGIONS OF LIGHT, GREAT ANGELIC HOST, GREAT COSMIC BEINGS AND GREAT COSMIC LIGHT!

Take complete command of the time of everyone under this Radiation forever! Use every moment in the Service of the Light! Make us always do the Perfect Thing, at the Perfect Time, in the Perfect Way for the Perfect Purpose, and expand the Ascended Masters' Full Perfection through us all forever.

✧ 85 ✧
VICIOUS APPETITES

"MIGHTY I AM PRESENCE," GREAT HOST OF ASCENDED MASTERS, MIGHTY LEGIONS OF LIGHT, GREAT ANGELIC HOST, GREAT COSMIC BEINGS, GREAT COSMIC LIGHT, AND ALL WHO GOVERN THE ACTIVITY OF THE GREAT QUENCHLESS FLAME OF DIVINE LOVE!

Annihilate the appetite in all humanity for narcotics, drink, tobacco, all flesh and excess food; that it may be released from this great barrier to Eternal Freedom! Replace these desires with the Ascended Masters' Satisfaction and Eternal enjoyment of the Almighty Perfection of the "I AM" and the abundance of every good thing! Produce by precipitation from the Universal Thy Perfect Food, that the bodies of mankind may be fed on Thy Pure Electronic Substance, express Thy Almighty Perfection, and become Self-luminous!

We ask the Mighty Cosmic Messengers also to take command! Prepare all the "I AM" Students, so we can walk and talk with You in Your Visible, Tangible, Living, Breathing Bodies from now on–in that Great Joy which all shall experience! We charge this Decree with Saint Germain, Jesus, Nada, and the Divine Director's Ascended Master Consciousness, Instantaneous Activity and Fulfillment, eternally sustained! We thank Thee it is done.

✧ 86 ✧

VIOLET FLAME

"MIGHTY BLESSED I AM PRESENCE," THOU SUPREME RULER OF THE VIOLET CONSUMING FLAME OF THE ASCENDED MASTERS' DIVINE LOVE! GREAT HOST OF ASCENDED MASTERS, MIGHTY COSMIC BEINGS, GREAT COSMIC LIGHT, AND MIGHTY LORDS OF THE FLAME FROM VENUS!

Blaze Thy Violet Consuming Flame up through us now, in Its most intense Activity, and cut away in One Mighty Sweep everything that binds or limits the Children of Light.

Mighty Angels of the Violet and Blue Lightning of Divine Love! Flash forth Thy Cosmic Power of the Blue Ray and consume from the atmosphere of Earth everything destructive, every humanly created entity! Purify all substance! Charge it with the Ascended Masters' Consciousness, Love, Light, and the Comprehension of the "I AM"! Let the Children of Light be so insulated within Its Almighty Purity and Perfection that no human suggestion of any kind can ever touch them or their worlds again. Project Thy Pillars of Violet Consuming Flame in, through, and around every human being on Earth, America and the world!

Blaze that forth with such Irresistible Consuming Power that all human creation, concepts, qualities, and activity of every kind shall be annihilated from within and around mankind, the Earth and its atmosphere, and their cause and effect be blasted from existence forever!

Make us all infinitely sensitive to Thee and Thy Perfection, and absolutely non-recordant to human creation! See that no person, place, condition or thing ever deceives us again, not even for the fraction of a second! See that the Children of Light are never surprised or off guard! that we never fail or make a mistake in a single thing! and that our beings and worlds are charged full to overflowing forever with Ascended Master Miracles and Victories in everything we do, instantly manifest and eternally sustained!

Release through the Children of Light, Power! Power! and more Power! the Almighty Power of Light and Love from the Ascended Masters! with such limitless energy, that all which is not of the Perfection of the Ascended Ones that dares to touch this Light, these Students of Light, anything in their worlds or under this Ascended Master Radiation knows instantly it has met its Master and annihilates itself forever!

The Power of Light and Love of the Ascended Masters shall so charge and insulate the Students of Light and all that they contact, that never again shall anything less than Perfection ever be expressed by them!

"The Light of God That Never Fails" now serves all who accept their "Mighty I AM Presence," and the Victory of that Light is *now*!

We thank Thee Thou dost always answer our every Call, instantly, infinitely and eternally! and we accept the full instantaneous action of this in everything we do, eternally sustained and ever-expanding!

✧ 87 ✧

WEATHER CONTROL

"MIGHTY I AM PRESENCE," GREAT HOST OF ASCENDED MASTERS, MIGHTY GOD TABOR!

Charge me (this room, Group, Class, city or country) with Thy Eternally Perfect Atmosphere, and keep me (or it) always *perfectly* comfortable at all times. Then make me radiate this same comfort to all I contact! I thank Thee Thou dost always answer my every Call, and this is eternally sustained and ever-expanding its Power!

✧ 88 ✧

WITHDRAW ALL DESTRUCTIVE WAR ACTIVITIES

"MIGHTY I AM PRESENCE," GREAT HOST OF ASCENDED MASTERS, MIGHTY LEGIONS OF LIGHT, GREAT ANGELIC HOST, GREAT COSMIC BEINGS, GREAT COSMIC LIGHT!

Come forth in Your most Dynamic Cosmic Action of the Violet Consuming Flame! Blast all destructive qualities and action from all war materials throughout the world forever! Annihilate their cause and effect in mankind, the Earth and its atmosphere for all Eternity! Seize all stored-up energy in those channels this very hour! Charge it with Saint Germain's and the other Ascended Masters' Consciousness of the "I AM," and blaze It through every human being, the Earth and its atmosphere, to create and maintain Ascended Master Protection and Perfection to all forever.

"Mighty I AM Presence"! Charge this our Decree with that Light and Love as of a Thousand Suns, and in the Full Activity of the Great Cosmic Light, send It forth to do Its Perfect Work forever.

✧ 89 ✧

WITHDRAW ALL ENERGY FROM DISCORD

"MIGHTY I AM PRESENCE," GREAT HOST OF ASCENDED MASTERS, MIGHTY LEGIONS OF LIGHT, GREAT ANGELIC HOST, GREAT COSMIC BEINGS, AND GREAT COSMIC LIGHT!

Come forth in Your most Dynamic, Almighty *Power* of the *Unfed Flame*! Withdraw and withhold *forever* all energy, money, power, supply, and influence from every discordant activity in America and the world! Annihilate their cause and effect from mankind and the Earth! Replace all such activities with the *Ascended Masters' Light Substance* and *Mighty Miracles of Perfection* instantly manifest everywhere, eternally sustained and ever-expanding! We thank Thee Thou dost always answer our every Call instantly.

✧ 90 ✧

YOUNG PEOPLE

"MIGHTY I AM PRESENCE," GREAT HOST OF ASCENDED MASTERS, MIGHTY LEGIONS OF LIGHT, GREAT ANGELIC HOST, GREAT COSMIC BEINGS, AND GREAT COSMIC LIGHT!

Blaze forth everywhere in, through, and around every young person on Earth the Mightiest Action of Your Sword of Blue Flame of Divine Love! Cut them free forever from everything that would bind them in any way to the limitations of human creation! or delay the full attainment of their Ascension in the Light of the "Mighty I AM Presence." Charge them with Invincible Ascended Master Purity, Protection, and Perfection, forever sustained! Seize and hold their attention wholly upon their own "Mighty I AM Presence" and the Ascended Masters forever! and charge them so full of *that Mighty Perfection* that never again can their attention be held by anything less than *Eternal Perfection! Use every moment of their time to expand Thy Full Perfection and Freedom through them to bless all! Release the Mighty Perfection of the "Golden Crystal Age"* through them to bring in the fulfillment of the *Ascended Masters' Divine Plan for America now,* and then expand *it* until It fills the Earth with Its Mighty Glory, eternally sustained and ever-expanding!

✧ 91 ✧

EMPLOYMENT
Individual and En Masse

"MIGHTY I AM PRESENCE" AND GREAT HOST OF ASCENDED MASTERS! Place every human being in Thy Perfect Channel of Employment or Activity! Show each one the Perfect Thing to do and make him do all *perfectly*! Release Thy lavish Supply of every good thing to all! See that they use it in the Service of the Light forever and set mankind Eternally Free.

We wish to thank all who give these Decrees for their assistance to America and their fellowman.

FINIS

THE
SAINT GERMAIN
SERIES